The Essential Buyer's Guide

MG
MGB & MGB GT

Your marque expert: Roger Williams

Essential Buyer's Guide Series

Alfa Romeo Alfasud (Metcalfe)
Alfa Romeo Alfetta: all saloon/sedan models 1972 to 1984 & coupé models 1974 to 1987 (Metcalfe)
Alfa Romeo Giulia GT Coupé (Booker)
Alfa Romeo Giulia Spider (Booker)
Audi TT (Davies)
Audi TT Mk2 2006 to 2014 (Durnan)
Austin-Healey Big Healeys (Trummel)
BMW Boxer Twins (Henshaw)
BMW E30 3 Series 1981 to 1994 (Hosier)
BMW GS (Henshaw)
BMW X5 (Saunders)
BMW Z3 Roadster (Fishwick)
BMW Z4: E85 Roadster and E86 Coupé including M and Alpina 2003 to 2009 (Smitheram)
BSA 350, 441 & 500 Singles (Henshaw)
BSA 500 & 650 Twins (Henshaw)
BSA Bantam (Henshaw)
Choosing, Using & Maintaining Your Electric Bicycle (Henshaw)
Citroën 2CV (Paxton)
Citroën DS & ID (Heilig)
Cobra Replicas (Ayre)
Corvette C2 Sting Ray 1963-1967 (Falconer)
Datsun 240Z 1969 to 1973 (Newlyn)
DeLorean DMC-12 1981 to 1983 (Williams)
Ducati Bevel Twins (Falloon)
Ducati Desmodue Twins (Falloon)
Ducati Desmoquattro Twins – 851, 888, 916, 996, 998, ST4 1988 to 2004 (Falloon)
Fiat 500 & 600 (Bobbitt)
Ford Capri (Paxton)
Ford Escort Mk1 & Mk2 (Williamson)
Ford Focus RS/ST 1st Generation (Williamson)
Ford Model A – All Models 1927 to 1931 (Buckley)
Ford Model T – All models 1909 to 1927 (Barker)
Ford Mustang – First Generation 1964 to 1973 (Cook)
Ford Mustang – Fifth Generation (2005-2014) (Cook)
Ford RS Cosworth Sierra & Escort (Williamson)
Harley-a Big Twins (Henshaw)
Hillman Imp (Morgan)
Hinckley Triumph triples & fours 750, 900, 955, 1000, 1050, 1200 – 1991-2009 (Henshaw)
Honda CBR FireBlade (Henshaw)
Honda CBR600 Hurricane (Henshaw)
Honda SOHC Fours 1969-1984 (Henshaw)
Jaguar E-Type 3.8 & 4.2 litre (Crespin)
Jaguar E-type V12 5.3 litre (Crespin)
Jaguar Mark 1 & 2 (All models including Daimler 2.5-litre V8) 1955 to 1969 (Thorley)
Jaguar New XK 2005-2014 (Thorley)
Jaguar S-Type – 1999 to 2007 (Thorley)
Jaguar X-Type – 2001 to 2009 (Thorley)
Jaguar XJ-S (Crespin)
Jaguar XJ6, XJ8 & XJR (Thorley)
Jaguar XK 120, 140 & 150 (Thorley)
Jaguar XK8 & XKR (1996-2005) (Thorley)
Jaguar/Daimler XJ 1994-2003 (Crespin)
Jaguar/Daimler XJ40 (Crespin)
Jaguar/Daimler XJ6, XJ12 & Sovereign (Crespin)
Kawasaki Z1 & Z900 (Orritt)
Land Rover Discovery Series 1 (1989-1998) (Taylor)
Land Rover Discovery Series 2 (1998-2004) (Taylor)
Land Rover Series I, II & IIA (Thurman)
Land Rover Series III (Thurman)
Lotus Elan, S1 to Sprint and Plus 2 to Plus 2S 130/5 1962 to 1974 (Vale)
Lotus Europa, S1, S2, Twin-cam & Special 1966 to 1975 (Vale)
Lotus Seven replicas & Caterham 7: 1973-2013 (Hawkins)
Mazda MX-5 Miata (Mk1 1989-97 & Mk2 98-2001) (Crook)
Mazda RX-8 (Parish)
Mercedes-Benz 190: all 190 models (W201 series) 1982 to 1993 (Parish)
Mercedes-Benz 280-560SL & SLC (Bass)
Mercedes-Benz G-Wagen (Greene)
Mercedes-Benz Pagoda 230SL, 250SL & 280SL roadsters & coupés (Bass)
Mercedes-Benz S-Class W126 Series (Zoporowski)
Mercedes-Benz S-Class Second Generation W116 Series (Parish)
Mercedes-Benz SL R129-series 1989 to 2001 (Parish)
Mercedes-Benz SLK (Bass)
Mercedes-Benz W123 (Parish)
Mercedes-Benz W124 – All models 1984-1997 (Zoporowski)
MG Midget & A-H Sprite (Horler)
MG TD, TF & TF1500 (Jones)
MGA 1955-1962 (Crosier)
MGB & MGB GT (Williams)
MGF & MG TF (Hawkins)
Mini (Paxton)
Morgan Plus 4 (Benfield)
Morris Minor & 1000 (Newell)
Moto Guzzi 2-valve big twins (Falloon)
New Mini (Collins)
Norton Commando (Henshaw)
Peugeot 205 GTI (Blackburn)
Piaggio Scooters – all modern two-stroke & four-stroke automatic models 1991 to 2016 (Willis)
Porsche 356 (Johnson)
Porsche 911 (964) (Streather)
Porsche 911 (991) (Streather)
Porsche 911 (993) (Streather)
Porsche 911 (996) (Streather)
Porsche 911 (997) – Model years 2004 to 2009 (Streather)
Porsche 911 (997) – Second generation models 2009 to 2012 (Streather)
Porsche 911 Carrera 3.2 (Streather)
Porsche 911SC (Streather)
Porsche 924 – All models 1976 to 1988 (Hodgkins)
Porsche 928 (Hemmings)
Porsche 930 Turbo & 911 (930) Turbo (Streather)
Porsche 944 (Higgins)
Porsche 981 Boxster & Cayman (Streather)
Porsche 986 Boxster (Streather)
Porsche 987 Boxster and Cayman 1st generation (2005-2009) (Streather)
Porsche 987 Boxster and Cayman 2nd generation (2009-2012) (Streather)
Range Rover – First Generation models 1970 to 1996 (Taylor)
Range Rover – Second Generation 1994-2001 (Taylor)
Range Rover – Third Generation L322 (2002-2012) (Taylor)
Reliant Scimitar GTE (Payne)
Rolls-Royce Silver Shadow & Bentley T-Series (Bobbitt)
Rover 2000, 2200 & 3500 (Marrocco)
Royal Enfield Bullet (Henshaw)
Subaru Impreza (Hobbs)
Sunbeam Alpine (Barker)
Triumph 350 & 500 Twins (Henshaw)
Triumph Bonneville (Henshaw)
Triumph Herald & Vitesse (Ayre)
Triumph Spitfire and GT6 (Ayre)
Triumph Stag (Mort)
Triumph Thunderbird, Trophy & Tiger (Henshaw)
Triumph TR2 & TR3 - All models (including 3A & 3B) 1953 to 1962 (Conners)
Triumph TR4/4A & TR5/250 - All models 1961 to 1968 (Child & Battyll)
Triumph TR6 (Williams)
Triumph TR7 & TR8 (Williams)
Triumph Trident & BSA Rocket III (Rooke)
TVR Chimaera and Griffith (Kitchen)
TVR S-series (Kitchen)
Velocette 350 & 500 Singles 1946 to 1970 (Henshaw)
Vespa Scooters – Classic 2-stroke models 1960-2008 (Paxton)
Volkswagen Bus (Copping)
Volkswagen Transporter T4 (1990-2003) (Copping/Cservenka)
VW Golf GTI (Copping)
VW Beetle (Copping)
Volvo 700/900 Series (Beavis)
Volvo P1800/1800S, E & ES 1961 to 1973 (Murray)

www.veloce.co.uk

First published in May 2006. Reprinted in April 2012 and November 2014. This edition first published October 2016 & reprinted November 2019 by Veloce Publishing Limited, Veloce House, Parkway Farm Business Park, Middle Farm Way, Poundbury, Dorchester, Dorset, DT1 3AR, England. Tel: 01305 260068. Fax 01305 250479/
e-mail info@veloce.co.uk/web www.veloce.co.uk or www.velocebooks.com
ISBN: 978-1-787116-55-9/UPC: 6-36847-01655-5

British Library Cataloguing in Publication Data – A catalogue record for this book is available from the British Library. Typesetting, design and page make-up al by Veloce Publishing Ltd on Apple Mac. Printed and bound by CPI Group (UK) Ltd, Croydon, CR0 4YY.

Introduction & thanks

– the purpose of this book

The purpose of this book is to offer a quick, step-by-step guide to finding an 1800cc MGB or MGB GT matched to your budget and ambitions. The task is often not as easy as it sounds, because owners' descriptions are, all too often, over-optimistic, and some cars have lots of problems hidden under their seductive exteriors.

Whatever the standard of car you seek, it will be out there, and finding it and helping you pay a fair price for it is the primary objective of the book. However, you need to start by making two decisions, the first of which is what are you prepared to pay? Clearly, it's pointless looking at cars beyond the price you are prepared to pay. Take care, however, for you need to crosscheck prices carefully using the various classic/collector car magazines, and by looking at several cars to ensure you've not set yourself an impossible task.

The UK magazine *Classic Cars* carries a monthly valuation review under the headings of Mint, Average and Rough, while *Practical Classics* also offers valuation information under Excellent, Regularly-used and Rebuild-required categories. The price guide in *Classic and Sports Cars* magazine is an excellent reference. You'll find similar magazines in other countries too. However, all these guides need to be used VERY carefully for at best they give an *average* figure for each category, and individual interpretations and valuations can vary by wide margins.

Nothing beats seeing cars, asking questions, and getting the feel of the market. Many vendors may rate you as a time waster if you give their car a 15-minute once over without buying, but it's essential you view a number of cars that seem to fall into your price and condition target before actually getting your money out of the bank! If you think you like what you see you can always take a few pictures and return to carry out a serious evaluation at a later date.

Along with the price issue is the related question of whether you're buying privately or from a dealer. How much redress do you want? Many buyers will be happy to pay more to a reputable dealer for the security of knowing that if anything goes wrong they can pick up the 'phone and get help. Buying from a private vendor may save you some money, but there is little redress and you are best advised to take this route only if you are confident (this book will be a huge help).

Particularly if going the 'private' route, be prepared to travel long distances and still be disappointed. There will be several frustrating trips where you feel the vendor was wasting your time, but the right car is out there and will make it all worthwhile when you find it, so be patient and persistent.

Whether the task is made easier or more difficult by the MGB's 28-year production run is debatable. It was in production from 1962 to 1980 – which must be amongst the longest production runs of all one-shape cars. Two models were available, and many components are interchangeable – the soft-topped Roadster was produced for all 28 years, and the Coupé or 'GT' variant for a large part of the production run. The popularity of open-topped classic motoring makes Roadsters the more sought-after, and results in their attracting higher market values.

However, the GT offers an excellent low-cost route to classic car motoring and should not be overlooked by first-time classic buyers.

Over half a million cars were produced as basically the same car – albeit in several different guises, the most obvious being the chrome and rubber bumper variations. However, the chrome bumper cars were produced in four different 'Series' and the rubber bumper models in two. Hidden under a very similar exterior, all the major components changed during the life of the car, as did the internal appearance. We will go into some of the main differences as this book develops, but you'll already appreciate that the MGB offers plenty of room for individuality. This is further extended by the vigorous aftermarket development work that has gone on since production ceased, generating arguably the widest variety of modifications and accessories for any car.

Thanks

I am indebted to the MG Car Club, and Peter Browning in particular, for invaluable factual and photographic support, without which this book would never have been produced.

Publisher's acknowledgement

We are indebted to Justin Banks who kindly provided many of the pictures used in the book. Justin's classic car sales company often has MGBs available to buy: www.godinbanks.com.

To the uninitiated, the MGB was produced in four models, two of which were the chrome bumper Roadster, seen here, and its GT variant. Both were offered with bolt-on wheels, or the highly desirable wire wheels seen on this 'Series III' car. This style of MGB is the most sought-after of all the MGBs. This car was first registered about 1971, but the traditional grille is from an earlier car.

The rubber bumper Roadster and its GT sister were introduced later, making four models in total. This GT is sporting the very desirable Wabasto full-length folding sunroof and, incidentally, a set of Minilite alloy road wheels.

Contents

Essential Buyer's Guide™ currency
At the time of publication a BG unit of currency "●" equals approximately £1.00/US $1.22/€1.11. Please adjust to suit current exchange rates.

1 Is it the right car for you?

– marriage guidance

Tall and short drivers

Standard seat adjustment is reasonable, and will accommodate all but exceptionally tall drivers – although drivers over 6 feet (1.85 metres) may find they have to look over the top of the windscreen/windshield frame in the Roadster.

Remembering that this is a sports car, the space within the cockpit is excellent.

Controls

The gearlever and pedals are nicely placed. The steering wheel and clutch pedal are easy to use, but by modern standards the brake pedal may seem slightly on the heavy side. The gearlever can be slightly 'notchy', particularly in worn examples, but has a commendably short throw. Handling is predictable and easy to control.

Will it fit the garage?

Length 3.89 metres/12ft 9¾in
Width 1.52 metres/4ft 11¾in

All the controls fall readily to hand: this car has a slightly smaller diameter, non-standard steering wheel for a quicker, but heavier, response.

Interior space

The cabin interior is spacious and excellent for a sports car. There is an abundance of legroom. Early Roadsters had a 'pack-away' hood frame which was stowed in the boot/trunk, but Roadsters with a folding hood frame lose about half the rear shelf space.

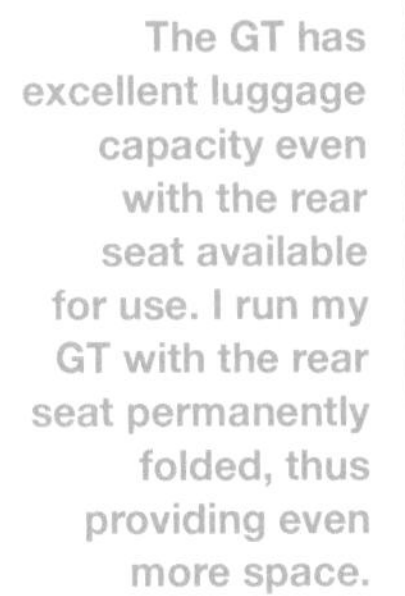

The GT has excellent luggage capacity even with the rear seat available for use. I run my GT with the rear seat permanently folded, thus providing even more space.

Luggage capacity

The standard spare wheel takes up much of the Roadster's otherwise large boot/trunk space and necessitates the use of soft bags. There is extra capacity on the rear shelf, accessed by fold-forward seats. The GT enjoys excellent luggage capacity, enhanced when the occasional rear seat is folded flat.

The boot/trunk of the Roadster is spacious without a spare wheel, but the wheel takes up about 35% of the space when carried.

Running costs

Modest. There is a comprehensive list of maintenance tasks at 6000 and 12,000 miles (10,000 and 20,000km) most of which are simple DIY tasks. However, it's best to grease the front suspension grease nipples every 3000 miles (5000km) and, if the car is little used, to change the engine oil and filter every 12 months.

Usability

Today, the Roadster should be regarded as a fun/second car rather than a daily driver for most owners, although a well-maintained GT can be used on a daily basis. Cars still fitted with the 3 main bearing engine are, in particular, definitely second cars/collectors' cars.

The rear seat of the GT is useful for occasional journeys but probably best for smaller members of the family. It folds flat to extend luggage capacity.

Parts availability

Numerous specialist suppliers on both sides of the Atlantic provide a full replacement parts service, ranging from new old stock (NOS), through rebuilt major components to complete new bodyshells.

Parts costs

See Chapter 2 for a more detailed list of new parts cost.

Insurance

Premiums can be quite modest if arranged through a recognised club scheme by an older driver with an exemplary record, but many factors affect the final cost.

Investment potential

Prices have been softening over the past couple of years, making it difficult for most owners to recover all buying and subsequent restoration costs. Better to buy a well-restored car, ideally built around a new bodyshell.

Foibles

Few.

Plus points

Timeless good looks, real character, popularity, and great top-down motoring (in a Roadster).

Minus points

The youngest MGB is at least 25 years old at the time of writing, so there are inevitably going to be unexpected problems, irritations, and repair bills.

Alternatives

To MGB Roadster – Alfa Romeo Spider, Triumph TR4, 4A, 6, 7 or Spitfire, Caterham 7, Mazda MX5.
To MGB GT – Triumph GT6, VW Scirocco, Toyota Celica, Porsche 924.

2 Cost considerations

– affordable, or a money pit?

Prices exclude taxes.

New mechanical parts

Clutch (set) x60
Front brake discs (each) x12
Front brake pads (kevlar) x28
Exhaust excluding manifold x125
Stainless manifold.... .... x120
Radiator (exchange). x80
Set water hoses x15
Alternator (exchange) x80
Distributor.... .... x92
Front shock absorbers (each) x60
Brake servo x145
Brake master cylinder.... .... x100
Rear brake shoes (set)... .... x15
Rear slave cylinder (each) x10
Clutch master cylinder... .... x45
Clutch slave cylinder x35
Cylinder head gasket x17
Unleaded cylyinder head x275
Reconditioned engine complete x950
Gearbox/transmission rebuild x300
Overdrive rebuild x275
Rear axle rebuild x300
Propeller shaft (new) x90
Fuel tank (new) x60
Fuel pump (electronic) x80
Carburettor service kit x37
Alloy wheels (each) x75

Body parts

Complete bodyshell (roadster) .. x3750
Front/rear wings/fenders (each) x250
Sill/rocker (set)... .... x130
Bonnet/hood x250
Door x200
Door skin x46
Boot/trunk lid x200
Windscreen/windshield.. .... x60
6-piece trim panel set – vinyl x80
Seat re-cover kit – vinyl.. .... x150
Moulded carpet set (roadster).... x145
New leather covered seats x700
New hood cover – vinyl.. .... x160
Pair new rear light clusters... .... x100

Rear brake with new shoes. It may be useful to point out that the adjuster is in full view at the top of the backplate, that this car has the highly advantageous telescopic dampers (yellow tube) fitted, and that this is the much sought-after wire-wheel hub.

Factory reconditioned engines came with a '48' prefixed engine number and were painted gold. Locally or specialist supplied refurbished engines will usually retain the original engine number, and will likely be finished differently.

Some of the replacement and/or repair panels on MGBs have subtle differences between early to late cars, but all cost about the same, and are, to my mind, remarkably low cost. In case you are wondering, these have been laid out to dry after the inside surfaces have been painted.

The rear light clusters come in two styles – albeit indistinguishable one from the other at a quick glance. This is the pre-1969 and less readily available style.

The MGB clutch set comprises 3 pieces. The cover (pressure plate) we see here has a friction plate trapped between it and the flywheel, while the clutch release (thrust bearing) attaches to the gearbox.

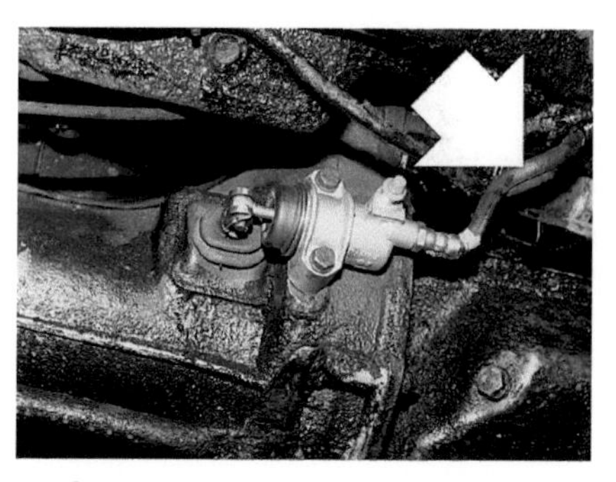

A new clutch slave cylinder shown attached to the side of the MGB gearbox. Always fit a new flexible hose (arrowed) at the same time as replacing the slave cylinder.

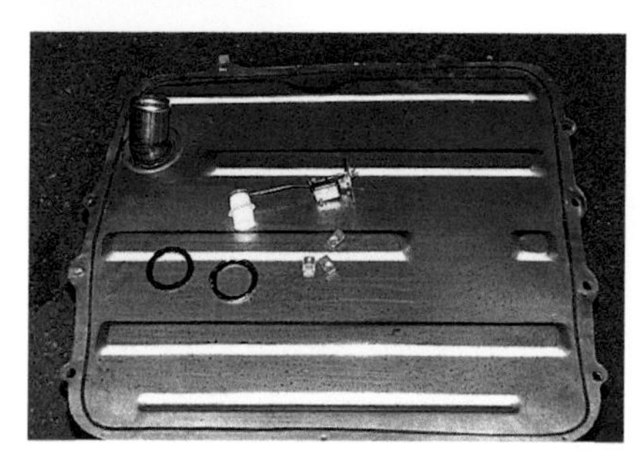

A stainless steel MGB fuel tank will cost more than the normal mild steel version, but is recommended as it will eliminate the possibility of future internal or external corrosion.

The latest replacement SU fuel pumps can come with a much improved electronic trigger, seen here with its protective cover removed. It's worth paying the extra cost for the electronic version.

3 Living with an MGB

– will you get along together?

One of the attractions of an MGB is that it is several cars in one – particularly the Roadster/open and Grand Turismo/Coupé variants. The Roadster is really only a two-seater, and much of the boot/trunk luggage space is taken up

Could you live with this beautifully restored 1965 Series I? So could I, although the rear shelf behind the front seats is as large as it gets. Later cars lost some of this space to a folding hood frame. Note the original leather seats.

The ever-popular Minilite wheels are lighter than the original wheels and thus improve road holding.

by a spare wheel. In contrast, the GT provides a (small) rear seat for two young children, and an impressive amount of

The sunroof on the GT makes the car a practical daily drive. This one, on this 1972 GT, is probably an aftermarket Britax item rather than an original dealer-fitted (as an optional extra) Wabasto unit.

The interior of an early car (about 1968-70 I would guess). The steering wheel is attractive, but non-original, as are the carpeted lower door trim panels.

luggage space (for a sports car) behind that. The load carrying capacity of both models can be increased. In the case of the Roadster you can substitute a 'space saver' spare wheel for the 5th road wheel and, in the case of the GT, you can fold the rear seat flat to extend the load deck forward – as is common in most modern hatchbacks.

The Roadster and GT are great fun to drive but the performance of the 105bhp variant (and this is the maximum) is very modest compared to modern sports cars. In fact, acceleration could be classed as ponderous, and the car is unlikely to out-perform a modern hatchback. However, they are far more individualistic than the modern hatchbacks, all of which appear to have come from the same mould. The Roadster is, however, probably best regarded as a second or 'high days and holidays' car, and this is particularly so for the early 'pull-handle' model.

One of the more common original wheels was the Rostyle. The body colour here is one of my favourites – Midnight Blue.

Depending upon what you're used to, the suspension will either feel hard or soft! Most readers will appreciate that the design of the front and rear suspension was regarded as 'traditional' when production of the MGB began in 1962, and probably 'ancient' when production ceased in 1980. If you've just jumped out of a TR7, or your power-assisted everything modern motor, you might find the MGB's ride or the controls 'agricultural'. My wife has used an MGB GT every day for several years and loves it. I have driven from the UK channel ports to the Pyrenees, South of France, Berlin, and numerous other far-flung corners of Europe – and enjoyed every minute of the journeys – so we find the ride perfectly acceptable. Better rear dampers improve the handling and precision with which the car can be driven, but the car is amazing considering the longevity of its design. The brakes, particularly when a servo is fitted, stop the car well, although at today's motorway speeds they can fade in standard form and I think benefit from relatively simple front calliper and disc/rotor upgrades.

The engine in later cars, particularly the rubber-bumper variants, became progressively strangled by anti-pollution equipment that reduced available power and the performance capabilities. The rubber bumpers are heavy and, as a result, further reduced performance capabilities of these later cars. Furthermore, the handling

Wire wheels, particularly chrome ones, really suit the MGB, but are very time-consuming to clean.

of the rubber bumper cars is inferior to their predecessors. Consequently, those who put performance at the top of their priorities prefer the pre-1974 cars while, coincidentally, most enthusiasts also prefer the aesthetics of the chrome bumper models.

However, remember that pre-October 1964 engines were fitted with only three main bearings. Right across the model range the gearbox was fitted with four forward speeds, but pre-1967 cars enjoyed synchromesh on only the top three ratios. Furthermore, these pre-1967 cars were fitted with dynamos (alternators were fitted as standard from 1967). So, to my mind, the preferred model years are post-1967 and pre-1974.

The early rubber bumper models (identified by the water radiator being 'tight' up to the front of the engine), including the 'Jubilee' edition, didn't have a rear anti-roll/sway bar fitted, and are, as a result, the worst handling MGB and best avoided.

It surprises most enthusiasts to learn how few MGBs were fitted with overdrive 5th gears. Today, overdrive is a necessity, not the highly desirable optional extra it once was, and a good car with overdrive will sell very quickly and at a premium, compared to a similar non-overdrive car.

Gear changes are clean and straightforward, if a little 'agricultural' or 'notchy'. However, it is not always appreciated that the gearbox should be filled with engine oil – NOT the EP gear oil that some owners assume. So, if you find the gearbox on the car you're testing is particularly difficult, it's worth casually inquiring what type of oil goes in the gearbox of an MGB. If the owner says "EP" or "gear oil" you may find that changing to a good quality 15/40 or 15/50 engine oil will transform the feel of the 'box.

Old cars are probably not best suited to owners unwilling to get their hands dirty from time to time. That said, I know several owners who know little about cars generally and get along with their 'Bs in perfect harmony – with the aid of an interested local garage. However, in general, when buying a 25 to 40-year-old car, it's better if you enjoy fiddling/fixing/maintaining cars, and the dirty hands (and satisfaction) that go with the work!

4 Relative values
– which model for you?

There is more detail on values in Chapter 12, but this chapter expresses, in percentages, the relative value of the individual models.

Chrome bumper Roadsters 1967-1974
5-bearing engine, 4-synchro gearbox
with overdrive - 100%
Non-overdrive - 90%

An example of the most desirable of the MGB range – a 1969 Roadster.

Chrome bumper Roadsters 1962-1967
Some with 3-bearing engines all with 3-synchro gearbox with
overdrive - 95%
Non-overdrive - 85%

Rubber bumper Roadsters 1974-1980
5-bearing engine, 4-synchro gearbox
with overdrive - 85%
Non-overdrive - 80%

The slightly earlier Series I Roadster – from 1965.

Chrome bumper GT 1967-1974
5-bearing engine, 4-synchro gearbox
with overdrive - 60%
Non-overdrive - 55%

Chrome bumper GT 1965-1967
5-bearing engines, 3-synchro gearboxes, some with
overdrive - 55%
Non-overdrive - 50%

Rubber bumper GT 1974-1980
5-bearing engine, 4-synchro gearbox
with overdrive - 50%
Non-overdrive - 45%

Furthermore –

- Many originally 3-bearing cars have been fitted with later 5-bearing engines. Some with non-original rear axles, door fittings and possibly seats – all in the name of improving the car. If you're

The last of the MGB models – a rubber bumper Roadster.

1972 GTs were amongst those MGBs produced with the recessed black grille.

This 1967 chrome bumper GT has been finished in a non-original body colour that sets off the wire wheels beatifully.

This rubber bumper GT is fitted with non-standard Wolfrace wheels.

comfortable with a non-standard car, then none of these variations will detract from the car's reliability, but if you're seeking originality or wish to enter concours competitions, then these changes will be unacceptable.

• There are a number of repatriated warm climate cars that come onto the UK market each year. Many remain in their original LHD condition, which devalues them. However, a number of these LHD cars have been converted to RHD. Even when the conversion has been carried out well, such cars do not attract quite the same value in the UK as an equivalent original RHD car. Where the conversion to RHD has been inexpertly carried out value will be further reduced.

• There are a number of Roadster models that are, in fact, conversions from a GT model, and retain their GT or Coupé chassis numbers and nomenclature on the registration documents. Their value is little more than their GT listing.

• There are numerous rubber bumper cars with conversions to chrome bumpers. Value these at their rubber bumper worth.

• The accompanying pictures should help you to distinguish one model from the next.

• A few cars were fitted with automatic gearboxes, which the majority of owners dislike, and such cars are reduced in value by as much as 10% compared with an equivalent specification manual car.

5 Before you view
– be well informed

To avoid the frustration of a car not matching your expectations, be sure to ask specific questions when you call before viewing. Excitement about buying an MGB can make even obvious things slip your mind, and it's harder for sellers to answer very specific questions dishonestly. Try to assess the attitude and demeanour of the seller, and decide how comfortable you are buying a used car from him or her.

Where is the car?
Work out the cost of travelling to view a car. For a rare model, or the exact specification you want, it may be worth travelling, but if your target is a common vehicle you should decide first how far you're prepared to go. Locally advertised cars can add to your knowledge for very little effort, so don't dismiss them.

Dealer or private sale
Is the seller the owner or a trader? Private owners should have all the history and be happy to answer detailed questions. Dealers may know less about a car, but should have some documentation and may offer finance. If a dealer offers no warranty or guarantee in writing, then consider if it's worth paying their higher price when you're geting little or no more protection than from a cheaper private sale?

Cost of collection and delivery
Dealers may deliver but it probably won't be cheap. Private owners may meet you halfway, especially if the car is roadworthy, but be sure to view the car at the vendor's address beforehand to validate ownership and vehicle documentation.

Viewing – when and where?
It's always preferable to view at the vendor's home or business. A private seller's name and address should be on the title documents unless there's a good reason why not. Have at least one viewing in daylight and preferably dry weather. Most cars look better in poor light or when wet.

Reason for sale
Genuine sellers will explain why they are selling and their length of ownership. They may also know something about previous owners.

Conversions and specials
Many MGBs have returned to Europe from the USA and other warmer climates. Some cars have been converted to RHD: some completely and invisibly, some with just the basics completed, leaving wipers, extra marker lights, carburettors, emissions equipment, compression ratio, perhaps even the headlamps unchanged.

To my mind a complete and invisible conversion need not affect a car's market value in the UK, but you need to be thinking ahead to the time when you wish to sell, because not every potential buyer may agree, particularly those seeking complete originality. There are some additional details included in Chapter 17, but the (red) commission number (fixed to the slam panel) on most pre-VIN cars will give you one clue. The fifth prefix letter on originally exported cars will either be an 'L' (signifying this was a LHD car) or a 'U,' signifying this was not only LHD but specifically made for the US market. Later cars with the more comprehensive VIN numbers also incorporate a telltale 3rd prefix letter coded as follows:

J = Japanese
L = Canadian
V = North America
Z = California

If you have any doubt, ask specific questions about the car's history and, where appropriate, its conversion, and that the lights in particular conform to local legislation.

Condition (body/chassis/interior/mechanics)

Query the car's condition in as specific terms as possible – preferably citing the checklist items described in Chapter 9.

All original specification

An unmolested original car is invariably of higher value and easier to get spares for than a customised vehicle.

Matching data/legal ownership

All MGBs have a car number (later called a VIN), commission number, body number, engine number and gearbox number. The body number plays no part in the normal identification process; indeed, it was usually discarded once the car was given its identification/VIN number. Early cars had no cross-reference with the car numberplate, although you can write to British Motor Heritage (Archives Department) for a 'Heritage Certificate' that usually gives most of the key component numbers. A changed engine number is fine if incorporated into the registration documents.

Does the vendor own the car outright or is money owed to a finance company or bank? Might the car be stolen? Do any necessary finance checks before buying. Some companies can often also confirm if the car has ever been an insurance write-off. In the UK, the following organisations can supply vehicle data:

DVSA	0300 123 9000
HPI	0845 300 8905
AA	0344 209 0754
DVLA	0844 306 9203
RAC	0800 015 6000

Other countries will have similar organisations.

Roadworthiness

Does the car have all necessary certificates and/or comply with emissions rules? MoT test status for UK cars can be checked by calling 0845 600 5977. Similar checks are available in some other markets.

If required, does the car carry a current road fund licence/license plate tag?

Unleaded fuel

As they left the factory all MGBs had what we now know as 'soft' valve seats which were unsuited to modern unleaded fuels. However, hardened inserts are now available and it has become common practice to have cylinder heads of this era converted for use with unleaded fuels, so you should ask whether the car you are viewing has been converted. If so, ask to see the receipt.

Do not overlook that MGB fuel lines around the carburettors and fuel pump include several lengths of flexible rubber hose – some stainless braided. These hoses, and any other flexible hoses you find in the fuel lines, are probably made from rubber that was not intended to carry modern aggressive unleaded fuels. These hoses need to be upgraded to unleaded-compatible rubber, with or without stainless braiding as appropriate.

Insurance

If intending to drive the car home, check with your existing insurer in case your current policy does not cover you. It's wise to check insurance costs before purchase in any case, as MGBs are valuable and quite fast cars.

How you can pay

A cheque/check will take several days to clear and the seller may prefer to sell to a cash buyer. Cash can also be a valuable bargaining tool. However, a banker's draft or money order may be as good as cash, so ask beforehand.

Buying at auction?

See Chapter 10.

Professional vehicle check

MGBs are not complex cars by today's standards. Nevertheless, there are some important checks that should be made. If you feel unsure about making these checks yourself there, there are often marque/model specialists who will undertake professional examination of a vehicle on your behalf. Owner's clubs will be able to put you in touch with such specialists.

Other organisations that will carry out a general professional check in the UK are:

AA 0800 056 8040 (motoring organisation with vehicle inspectors)
RAC 0330 159 0720 (motoring organisation with vehicle inspectors)

Other countries will have similar organisations.

6 Inspection equipment

– these items will really help

This book

This book is designed to be your guide at every step, so take it along and use the check boxes in Chapter 9 to help assess each area. Don't be afraid to let the seller see you using it.

Glasses (if needed)

Take your reading glasses if you need them to read documents and make close up inspections.

Magnet (not powerful, a fridge magnet is ideal)

A magnet will help you check if the car is full of filler, or has fibreglass panels, but be careful not to damage the paintwork. It is a rule of MGBs that the rust you see is always far less than the hidden rust you cannot see. There's nothing wrong with a fibreglass bonnet/hood or boot/trunk lid apart from the reduced value and sometimes paint finish. You will find the magnet particularly useful at the point where body panels meet. See Chapters 7 and 9 for a more comprehensive breakdown of locations particularly vulnerable to corrosion, and where, consequently, body filler is popular.

Probe (a small screwdriver works very well)

A small screwdriver can be used – with care and the owner's consent – as a probe, particularly on the inner and outer sills/rockers, rear lower quarters, boot/trunk floor, and anywhere around the bulkhead and battery tray to check areas of corrosion.

Overalls

Be prepared to get dirty and ideally take some overalls for getting under the car.

Mirror on a stick

Fixing a mirror at an angle on the end of a stick can help check the condition of the underside of the car and some of the important areas around the chassis. You can also use it, together with a torch, at several points on the chassis and bodywork detailed in Chapters 7 and 9. A full on-ramp inspection is ideal.

Digital camera

If possible, take a digital camera for reference or to study known trouble spots later. Show an expert pictures of any part that causes you concern. Ideally, have a friend or knowledgeable enthusiast accompany you: a second opinion is always valuable.

7 Fifteen minute evaluation
– walk away or stay?

How does it go/sound/feel

Assuming your insurance covers you, go for a short run. Do not worry about the tune, acceleration or finer details – we're initially looking for expensive-to-fix problems. The car must pull up straight on the brakes, not puff out smoke from the exhaust, change gear without bulking or grating, and steer straight 'hands-off' the steering wheel. Obviously, you also need to ensure there are no unpleasant noises or 'clonks' from the front suspension (a common fault), engine, gearbox or rear axle areas of the car when accelerating, braking or turning.

Try the gearbox briefly in each of the four gears, concentrating for now on testing each gear on over-run. The gear should stay engaged but if it pops out the gearbox is worn. If overdrive is fitted, try flicking the 'in' switch with the car in top gear at about 50mph/80kph – it should snap into operation. They always drop out quickly so that's no test, but a worn overdrive will usually take a few seconds to get up to pressure after the switch has been flicked 'in,' which signals remedial cost in due course.

Any whine from the rear axle on drive or over-run?

Try as many electrical switches as possible in the time available – the reflection in a shop window is sometimes helpful to confirm things are working.

Check the engine oil pressure towards the end of the run – it should be at least 50psi at about 2500rpm.

You'll get a good idea of how evenly curved the two sides of the car are from the rear. This view will also help you see any major ripples in the panels. These are the post-1969 rear light clusters.

Exterior

An overall impression of the bodywork is best obtained from the rear of the body. Go to one rear corner and kneel down to sight down the coach line. The car should have a steady curve without significant ripples in any panel (which would signal a knock and/or poor rebuild).

Stand out to both sides and look at the chrome coach line. The three pieces should all line up, forming one straight line, and they should be level with the road – that is the front strip should be at the same height from the road as the rear strip – both sides.

Check that the car sits level on the road and that the chrome coach line is at equal height front and rear.

If in doubt, measure them. Chances are the car will sit 'tail-down' and need new rear springs.

Check each of the panel gaps with the adjoining 'fixed' panel – in particular, the door gaps with the adjoining B post. These gaps should be even right the way up the height of each rear door edge. If one or both the gaps close toward the top, chances are the sills/rockers are corroded and have lost much of their integrity. Potential Roadster owners can push down hard on the front of the rear wing/fender (where the hood frame is mounted) and watch for further (slight) movement in the door gap, which would confirm the unsound nature of the sill/rocker(s). GT viewers will need to look under the car for confirmation of a structural problem.

Few GTs should have door gap problems, but the door gaps on Roadsters can taper, the doors even binding at the top. Be very wary of any such cars.

You'll get an impression of the extent to which rust has progressed throughout the bodywork if you check the following areas for rust, paint bubbling, body filler (use a magnet if unsure), or signs of remedial attention:

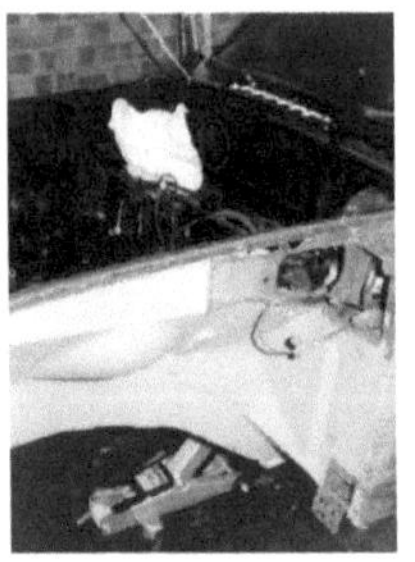

The corrosion in this normally out of sight but structurally important panel was so bad I had to replace the whole tapered/wedge-shaped piece. You can see the outline of the original 'wedge' and the corrosion eating into the inner wing panel above. You must feel (carefully) and look as well as you are able before buying.

- the four wing/fender panel joints where each panel meets the scuttle at the front and the rear deck at the back.
- along the bottom of the doors.
- under the front wings.
- the exterior and interior of the sills/rockers (where they join the floor) – look particularly closely near the A posts and the jacking point.

An example of corrosion at a panel junction which probably signals panel deterioration underneath – this is bad news and can occur in any of the vulnerable places mentioned throughout this book.

While you're making these checks, take a few seconds to survey the overall quality of the paintwork, and whether you like the colour.

Lastly, check the bumpers for damage – rubber for tears and/or fading, chrome for rust and/or dents.

Under-bonnet/hood

Lift the bonnet/hood and check the wing/fender gutter joints for corrosion (bad news) and for signs of a soft sealer having been coated on the panel faces before the wing/fenders were bolted to the shell (good news). Check that the under-bonnet/hood paintwork matches the exterior paint colour, and look closely for corrosion around the area where the fusebox is mounted. Don't forget to make an identical check on the other side of the car.

While you've got your head in the engine bay and have

torch in hand, make a note of the engine number and take a quick look round the engine bay for any signs of water and/or oil leaks.

If the engine prefix does not match the supposed origin of the car, the 'originality' value can be adversely affected, but maybe, in some cases, not severely. On occasions, similar engines from Morris Marinas have been installed and this will considerably devalue the car. Early 3-bearing engines have often been replaced with a later, and stronger, 5-bearing MGB engine. Only you, the buyer, can decide whether you see that as an advantage or disadvantage.

Check the splash plates at the back of each front wheelarch. You can usually see any major corrosion at the bottom of the splash plates, but you might need to feel (very carefully) for the condition of the plate that goes across the top of the rear of the wheelarch, and whether the respective rubber seals are in place and have prevented water accessing the (hidden) area behind the front wing/fender. A second, but equally vulnerable, area is across the top of the triangular gusset above the splash plate for, if holed, this allows water and thus corrosion into the top rear of the engine bay, behind the fusebox.

At the rear of the car, lift the boot/trunk lid and, using your torch, look first, then very carefully run your hand over the outer edges of the inner wheelarches as far forward as you can. You are looking/feeling for corrosion and/or body filler! While you're there, partially lift the spare wheel and take a look at the floor of the boot/trunk – which is very vulnerable to corrosion.

Underneath

With your safety at the forefront of your mind, look at the inside faces of the sills and chassis crossmembers by driving the rear of the car up onto a pair of ramps, or by jacking the rear of the car and securely placing axle stands under it. Take your torch and, if the current owner agrees, a small prodder (a screwdriver is ideal) and examine the inside faces of the sills/rockers, the bottoms of the two channel sections that run front to rear under the floors, and the one channel that runs across the shell. You must be sure the main chassis members are free of serious corrosion and/or patched repairs. The best test of the sills/rockers (only if the owner agrees) is to get the car back on the road and, making absolutely sure you are clear of the car at all times, fit the car's jack in the jacking point below the centre of the sill. A solid sill and jacking point will allow you to raise each side of the car sufficiently to, say, change a wheel. A weakened sill will probably creak and groan a warning, while a corroded and unsatisfactory sill will almost certainly allow the jacking point to go through into the sill and signal it's time to walk away.

If you have the car up on ramps, take the opportunity to look at the front mounting points of both rear springs, the underside of the boot/trunk floor, and the rear face of the rear valance.

Take a look at the front face of the fuel tank. You may not see any significant corrosion, but look out for (and sniff) streaks resulting from a fuel leak from the hidden top of the fuel tank. If the tank is full of fuel, take great care because a hot light, such as a mains-powered lead-lamp, can actually ignite fuel droplets. Use a battery-powered torch/flashlight in this area.

Interior

Take a quick look underneath the doors, lift the carpets in the footwells and check the four outer corners of the floors. Look at the trim panels and carpets, but don't place too much importance on their appearance.

This door is perfect, having been recently restored, but the bottom of the frame, outer skin, and inner trim panel are all vulnerable to water damage and corrosion.

Mechanics

How does the engine sound on tick-over/idle? The MGB engine is quite noisy so expect there to be some churning, tapping, and a little rattling. Take advice if it's excessive, but replacement engines are not horrendously expensive.

Paperwork

If you're still interested, this would be a good moment to check the registration document – the V5C in the UK and the Pink slip in the USA. Only buy a car from an individual who can prove that they are the person named in the car's registration document (V5C in the UK) and, preferably, at the address shown in the document. Check that the chassis number and engine numbers not only crosscheck with the registration document, but are also compatible with the year of the car and its model number. You will find this information in Chapter 17.

A lot of work has clearly gone into the exterior of this car but the life-expectancy of this floor worries me, in that superficial corrosion is obvious but I think I can see more serious corrosion where the floor joins the sill/rocker.

Is it worth staying for a longer look?

• Is the colour what you expected or can live with?
• Does the paintwork seem acceptable?
• Does the bodywork seem sound – bearing in mind that a body and paint restoration is very expensive?
• Can you rectify the problems you've noticed, or should you take advice about what is involved before you decide?
• Although the easiest and least expensive to rectify, are the main mechanical components in reasonable order so far?
• Are the problems you've discovered reflected in the price?
• Is your heart ruling your head? Take time to think, and perhaps talk to an MGB professional/specialist. Best not to act in haste and repent at leisure!

This 1972 car looks superb, and you can see the rectangular 'rocker' switches and radio console that were introduced that year. Earlier switches were 'toggles,' fitted into circular holes in the dashboard. From 1972 on, expect the radio to be fitted in the radio console, and the higher dashboard aperture to be fitted with a pair of face-level air vents.

8 Key points
– where to look for problems

The colour and quality of the paint finish is very important. Note the 'knock-on' Minilites that fit on wire wheel hubs, and the excellent taut hood.

Note the uniform panel gaps round the boot/trunk lid, the excellent chrome, and the pre-1969 light cluster.

Wheels can change the appearance of a car dramatically. These original Rostyle wheels may not be 'sexy', but they're very practical.

The quality and colour of the paintwork in the engine bay will give you some idea of how well a car has been restored. This car is a 1972 model – thus the carburettors are SU HS4 type. The rocker cover and K&N aftermarket air filters are non-standard, but welcome changes.

The traditional and most popular of MGB grilles – the original 'vertical bar' version.

This recessed radiator grille did not prove popular and lasted only from 1969 to 1972. The black rubber faces fitted to the over-riders were introduced in 1971 and were replaced by complete rubber bumpers in 1974. The extra driving lights are a good idea and should not adversely affect cooling.

Ensure the alloy windscreen/windshield frame on the Roadster is in good order.

The frame surrounding the GT 'screen is equally important.

This pre-1968 example shows a pair of standard HS4 SU carbs with non-standard air cleaners. A fuel filter has been fitted.

Left: This 1972 GT 'Autumn Leaf' interior trim looks exemplary. Post-1972 cars were fitted with a steering lock (what seemed like) deep in the footwell! You can just see the ignition key to the left of the gear knob.

9 Serious evaluation

– 60 minutes for years of enjoyment

It's hard to remember all the details of a car you inspect, even an hour or two later, so circle the Excellent, Good, Average or Poor box of each section as you go along. The totting up procedure is detailed at the end of the chapter. Be realistic in your marking.

Paintwork

Like bodywork shortcomings, paintwork can be very expensive to properly correct. It takes time to remove all chrome work, and perhaps the front wings/fenders and fittings, and to effect the chemical strip to bring the car back to bare metal. Then there's hours of repairing, filling and rubbing down; all before the actual painting can take place. It takes time to do the complete job properly, and you are, as a result, looking at spending a lot of cash to have the paintwork applied properly to an existing car. Even new Heritage or rust-free Californian shells may need to have the front wings/fenders removed before painting in order to ensure that sealant fully covers the mating (water trap) surfaces when re-assembled.

You can save some money by doing the stripping yourself, but good paint will pay for itself in time, though it's expensive in the short term. You also need to view a car that has been repainted fairly recently with a jaundiced eye, and ask yourself 'what filled-in corrosion weaknesses has the paint covered up?'

Body panels

The most expensive part of an MGB to repair/restore is the bodywork. The worst case scenario would be to buy a car requiring extensive repairs or a replacement bodyshell – so take all the time you need to satisfy yourself that the car you're looking at isn't going to need expensive body restoration in the near future. Sadly, it's an inescapable fact that all MGBs have a number of corrosion weak spots. You must be alert to filler cover-ups anywhere in the car, but particularly in the weak spots listed. Each location should be examined carefully, and a magnet used to test for body filler when in doubt (if filler is present a weak magnet will not adhere). Speaking of body filler, there used to be a tendency to mask corrosion by filling the gaps between some body panels, particularly at the rear of the car. Regard any car where there is no clear and obvious seam between each wing and its mating panels with suspicion.

Door shut lines

MGB door gaps close at the top as the chassis structure weakens – so tapered gaps are bad news, particularly along the rear verticals, and should alert you to question the integrity of the bodyshell. Be particularly wary of a car where either door is difficult to open and/or close. Push down on top of the rear wing/fender and walk away if the top gap closes.

Door shut lines appear even from here, but a closer look is advisable.

Bonnet/boot shut lines 4 3 2 1

Take a close look at the evenness of the gaps between bonnet/hood to wing/fender, bonnet to scuttle, boot lid to rear wing/fender, and boot lid to rear deck. They should all be even and consistent.

The front valance/apron is susceptible to corrosion, kerbs/curbs and other raised objects, and to accident damage; body filler is often present, masking its true condition. On its own it is easy and cheap to replace.

The front valance is attacked from front and rear, and suffers accordingly. Note the quite severe corrosion down the bonnet/hood gutter, probably hidden until the wing/fender was removed.

Chrome strip 4 3 2 1

Check down the length of each chrome strip, as the mounting holes in the panels encourage corrosion, which you'll see as paint bubbling in spots along the trim.

Front wings/fenders (7 checks) 4 3 2 1

• Around the headlamps, particularly where the chrome trim attaches to the wing.

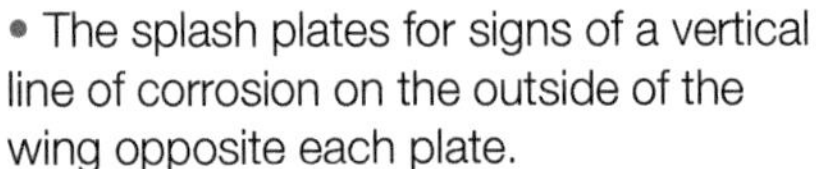

• The splash plates for signs of a vertical line of corrosion on the outside of the wing opposite each plate.

• The scuttle panel mating areas.

• Pull the bonnet release toggle. It will require a firm pull with two fingers, but should not be stiff, nor the mechanism/cable seized.

• Inside the engine bay, by the fusebox on the inner wing and, of course, on the opposite side of the car, too. Repair is time-consuming and expensive.

• Under the top/rear of each wing/fender there is a tapered box panel. These corrode across the top first: if corrosion is very serious the whole stress-bearing box can disintegrate: an expensive repair.

• The lower front wing in front of the sill/rocker.

Look right along the chrome strip for corrosion ...

... like this. It's always worst at the front and where the clip securing holes come through each panel. It is exacerbated here by corrosion around the headlamp.

These are new splash plates with, note, a rubber seal to prevent water getting in behind.

This tapered box panel was sufficiently corroded to warrant replacement.

Doors

4 3 2 1

Sadly, rust can be obvious without the need to check with a magnet, but if the doors look OK superficially still make five checks –

• Run your hand carefully along the bottom where the door shell joins the outer skin.

• The bottom few inches (say 100mm) of outer door skin needs checking for body filler.

• Both door skins below the quarter-light are prone to splitting.

• With the door half open, lift it up, feeling for wear in the hinges.

• Feel the bottom of the door trim panel for softness/warping due to water ingress from inside the door.

The sills/rockers

4 3 2 1

Corrosion on the outside is usually obvious and normally visible, though the front wing/fender covers the first couple of feet and, as a result, the sill/rocker can be disintegrating but hidden from the outside of the car. Check along the inner sill/rocker and floor panel – particularly at the outer front corners.

This sill/rocker panel doesn't look unduly corroded at first glance ...

... until the outer sill panel is removed to reveal the true extent of the damage.

Inside the cockpit

4 3 2 1

This carpet looks fine but it is, nevertheless, worth peeling it back or removing it for a look at the floor itself.

• The floors in the cockpit generally, but particularly at the four corners nearest each of the wheels.

• Wet/damp carpets, which could bring you to suspect the plenum chamber is corroded. This double-skinned cavity goes across the full width of the car under the scuttle/windscreen, and if the drain gets blocked it can hold water, which then enters the air vent. Water on carpets and/or rust on the floor panels should lead you to check under the dashboard. This is a difficult and expensive repair.

• Do the seats slide and lock easily? Reluctance to slide can be due to poor lubrication and/or lack of use, but can also signal a weak/sagging floor.

Rear wing/fender

4 3 2 1

There are three specific areas to check –

• Around the wheelarch lip (where it's welded to the inner wing).

• The bottom of the rear light cluster.

• The panel seams to the top and to the rear of the rear wing panel – these are frequently filled to mask corrosion.

This is the top bead of the rear wing – not looking good.

Rear inner wing

4 3 2 1

Check for corrosion from both:

- Outside the car.
- Inside the boot/trunk by looking at and feeling the inner wings/fenders. The inside of the GT wheelarch will be covered with carpet, so check the carpet for dampness, and the integrity of the underlying metal by pushing in selected spots.

Boot/trunk floor

4 3 2 1

You may need to remove the spare wheel, but the floor is vulnerable to corrosion.

This is a new boot/trunk floor – note the surrounding sealer and the surface corrosion on the rear panel.

Rear valance

4 3 2 1

Run your hand (carefully) along the entire bottom edge of the rear valance (particularly where the exhaust pipe exits) to check for corrosion masked by filler. You will get a hint from the condition of the adjacent boot/trunk floor.

Boot/trunk lid

4 3 2 1

Two checks:

- For corrosion in the seam along the bottom of the tailgate on a GT, and along the bottom lip of the boot/trunk lid on Roadsters.
- Later Roadsters had a telescopic lid support on the left side – check for cracking in the boot lid around the top mounting bracket.

The windscreen frame (GT only)

4 3 2 1

Check the paintwork for signs of corrosion around the perimeter of the windscreen/windshield, but particularly in the bottom corners.

The screen weakness on the GT is at the base of the pillars. Corrosion is just starting here. The door gap looks wrong.

Seating comfort

4 3 2 1

How do the seats support your back? Do the seat back (squab) cushions feel firm and supportive? Are the base cushions firm, or do they feel as if they are unsupported and/or the foam disintegrating, not giving you a firm seat?

This rubber diaphragm forms the base of the seat and, with age, collapses.

Later bases were made from webbing, but these stretch and collapse, too.

Start-up

Cold start

4 3 2 1

- Make a mental note of the car's cold starting characteristics as you start it for the first time (is it swift and effortless, or a long grind?).

• On start-up, does the car puff blue smoke? This would indicate general wear and 'tiredness'.

The rocker shaft (across the top of the picture) and rockers wear and, subsequently, rattle.

Engine noises – three checks

4 3 2 1

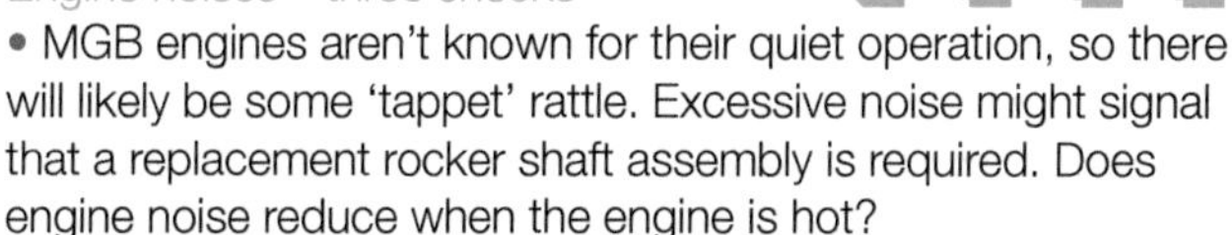

• MGB engines aren't known for their quiet operation, so there will likely be some 'tappet' rattle. Excessive noise might signal that a replacement rocker shaft assembly is required. Does engine noise reduce when the engine is hot?

• Rocker shafts are easy and inexpensive to replace, but any 'rumbling' from the bottom end would indicate a completely different level of expense.

• Listen for a light 'tinkling' sound. This would suggest a stretched/tired timing chain and, possibly, worn sprockets. If all three noises are present, budget (and negotiate later) for a service-exchange engine – particularly if you note oil leaks later in your examination and/or puffs of blue smoke. If the engine is noisy or smoky, it may be time to walk away.

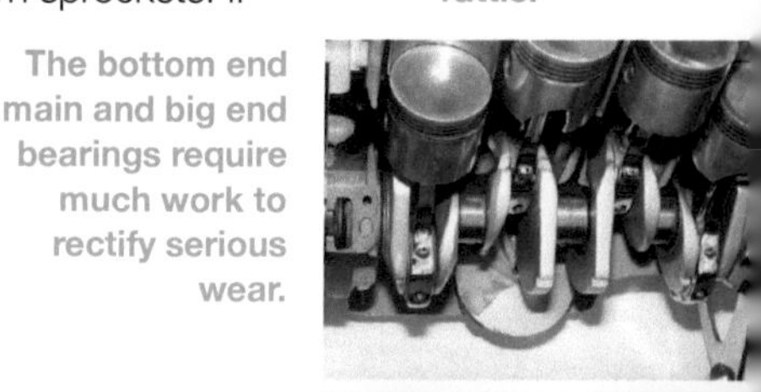

The bottom end main and big end bearings require much work to rectify serious wear.

Still there? Then it's time to check the structural integrity of the car.

The timing chain can stretch with prolonged use.

Checking under the car

Unless you're exploring a very cheap restoration candidate, it's worth pre-arranging a half hour session on the lift at a local garage. You can then check the following in safety, and without having to scrabble around on the ground. If you're forced to look under the car at home, do so with the car safely chocked and on a pair of service ramps, or properly supported on axle stands.

Underside structure

4 3 2 1

Probe (with a small screwdriver) and look for corrosion and/or patching in the following ten places, each side of the car –

• The jacking points, roughly central to the sill/rocker.
• The jacking point to jacking point crossmember.
• The insides of the front and rear valances.
• The fixed rear spring hanger and surrounding metalwork.
• The chassis leg at the pivoting shackle rear spring mounting.
• The rear wheelarches.
• The boot/trunk floor.
• The fuel tank, particularly at the top and front, for streaks and/or other signs of escaping fuel.
• The battery cradles (chrome bumper cars have two).

This jacking point looks in good order after a recent repair but ...

... this crossmember looks less convincing.

This is the foremost of the two rear spring hangers ...

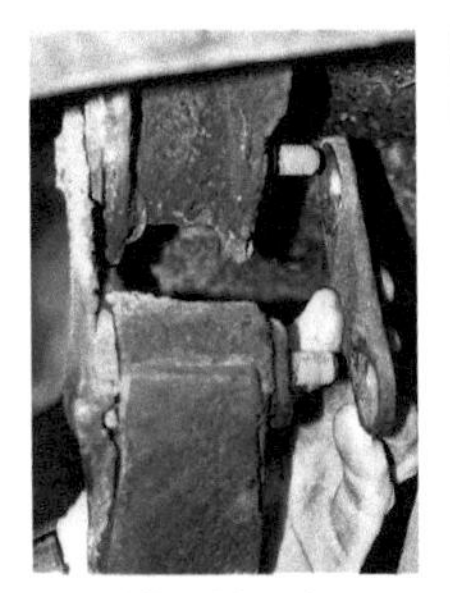

... while this picture shows the chassis member that supports the rear of the spring.

Wet mud accumulates on the front of the fuel tank and eventually corrodes it.

• Last, but certainly not least, check that the chassis members and underside of the body show evidence of internal and external wax protection.

Rear axle/wheel/brakes – two checks each side

4 3 2 1

• It's particularly important to test for spline/hub 'play' in wire-wheeled cars. Apply the hand/parking brake and jack one rear wheel just clear of the ground. Try to spin each road wheel in turn listening/feeling for clonks which signify that the wheel and axle spline are worn (expensive to rectify).

• Check the rear of the brake drum, and the inside of the wheel for oil leaks that signify a worn oil seal, or (less serious) a blocked breather atop the differential.

This oil leak is plain to see, but might not be so obvious with the wheel on.

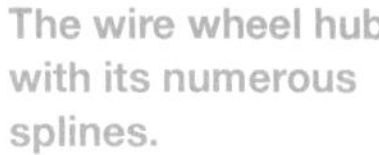

The wire wheel hub with its numerous splines.

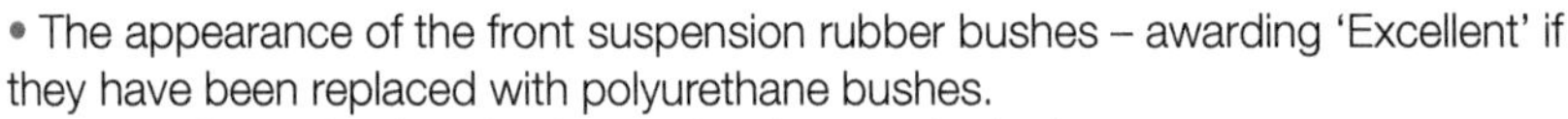

Front suspension – four checks each side

4 3 2 1

• The appearance of the front suspension rubber bushes – awarding 'Excellent' if they have been replaced with polyurethane bushes.

• Raise a front wheel under the road spring pan in the lower

The suspension bushes are located at the outer end of the top arm, and at both ends of the bottom arm. No sign of coloured polyurethane bushes here!

You will not see this view with the essential dust cap in place, but with it removed the outer wheel bearing is (more or less) revealed.

wishbone. Turn that wheel while feeling and listening for roughness in the wheel bearings.

• Grasp the wheel top and bottom and rock the wheel hard, feeling for *excessive* 'play' in the wheel bearing (there needs to be slight play), the wire wheel splines (if applicable), and the all-too-frequent MGB problem, kingpin and lower outer bush wear. If suspicious, you might be able to double-check the kingpin and bush wear by using a tyre lever (or similar bar) under the bottom of the tyre in order to move the hub up and down (this is very difficult if the car is not on a proper garage ramp).

• Look for evidence of recent attention to the three grease nipples per kingpin (it's vital that these are frequently greased if the MGB kingpin wear problem is to be prevented).

Frequent greasing of the front suspension is essential for longevity.

Steering – four checks

4 3 2 1

• Check the obvious steering components (rack and balljoints) for wear, and the integrity of the various gaiters when rocking the steering back and forth.

• If more than ¾in (20mm) movement is detected at the steering wheel rim when the road wheels remain stationary, look and feel for play in the steering column universal joint just in front of the bulkhead/firewall.

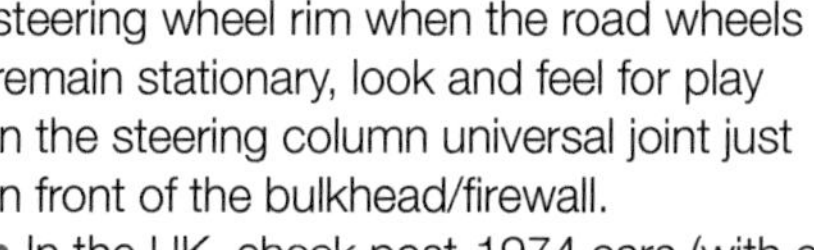

The steering ball joints and gaiters will need checking.

• In the UK, check post-1974 cars (with collapsible steering columns) to ensure there is no significant play between the inner column and outer mounting tube.

• Turn the steering wheel lock-to-lock, with the front wheels slightly raised, feeling for roughness that signals a worn steering rack.

Shock absorbers

In practice you can only visually check the four dampers. You can try bouncing each corner of the car up and down, but only completely useless dampers will be revealed by this 'test'.

• Rear – Award 'Excellent' marks if telescopic replacements have been recently fitted. If the original 'lever arm' rear dampers are in place, check both for oil leaks at each end of the pivot (where it enters the housing).

• Front – Same bounce check.

This is the original 'lever arm' rear damper off the car ...

... while this is the much more desirable telescopic, but non-original upgrade.

The front original lever arm dampers need checking.

Propeller shaft

Check both prop shaft u/js for wear/play.

There are two to check, but the rear propshaft universal joint is just the far side of the box spanner.

Oil leaks – four checks are worthwhile 4 3 2 1

• The differential front seal. Don't worry about the normal slight weep, but if oil has been thrown onto the underside of the body, mark this as requiring repair.
• The gearbox rear seal.
• The drain hole in the bellhousing will always have evidence of oil weep, but look for excessive amounts that could emanate from a leaking front gearbox seal or the engine's rear crankshaft seal. Clean oil may be from the gearbox, but carbon laden oil will certainly be from a leaking rear engine seal. If the engine is a 5-bearing unit then a new lip seal might be necessary, and costs very little, but requires a costly engine removal. However, if the engine is a 3-bearing early unit, you have a dilemma. The scroll always leaks to some extent, but you may be looking at a badly worn scroll that necessitates a replacement engine. Judge and mark accordingly.
• The front cover seal can leak due to excessive crankcase pressure (consequence of blocked evaporative control system), but assume a new seal is required.

Exhaust system

Check the exhaust system for corrosion, sound-looking joints, and appropriate mountings. If in doubt, test it by having the engine run while you listen for 'blows'. Only mark as 'Excellent' if a good stainless-steel system is fitted.

Test drive

Assuming you're properly insured, take at least thirty minutes over this, as it's a good opportunity to assess the car's driving characteristics.

Gearbox assessment – four checks

• With the car stationary and the engine running, try selecting each gear. It will require full depression of the clutch, but the gearlever should not refuse, nor should it make any complaining noises.
• At about 45mph in third, and subsequently in fourth gear, swiftly lift off the accelerator/gas to see if the gearlever jumps out of gear, signalling worn selectors.
• At about 30mph in third gear, try changing into second. It might be slightly notchy, but shouldn't be very difficult (which would signal a worn clutch), nor generate crunching noises. Difficult and noisy warns you that the synchromesh cones are worn.
• Stop in a quiet spot and listen while you slowly drive forward in first gear. If the gearbox hisses then it's likely that the layshaft needle roller bearings are picking-up on the layshaft's hardened surface, and will require replacement in due course. This

is particularly bad news if the car is fitted with overdrive, for not only is it essential to overhaul the gearbox, but the overdrive unit, too.

The clutch/pedal

4 3 2 1

Four checks here, all with the car stationary on a hill and the engine running

- Does first gear engage reasonably easily? If not, the clutch is probably worn.
- With the car in second gear, let the clutch pedal up slightly slower than normal until the engine slows. If the engine hardly slows and/or the car hardly moves forward, the clutch is worn and requires the engine to come out for a replacement clutch.
- Does the pedal 'bite' about halfway up its travel and is it consistent? Be alert for wear in the master and slave forks/ clevis pins (a common occurrence) and, more seriously, a worn carbon clutch thrust release pad.
- Does the clutch engage smoothly without judder?

This clutch pressure plate can wear, but it is the friction plate inside that causes the majority of clutch problems. You need the engine out to effect a repair here.

A worn clevis pin and arm can adversely affect the clutch, and is an easy, low-cost repair, but sadly ...

... the same cannot be said for this clutch thrust pad, which requires the engine out to replace.

Overdrive operation

4 3 2 1

With the car in fourth gear at about 50mph, flick on the overdrive control switch. Overdrive (if fitted) should cut in immediately and with sufficient force to slightly jolt you. Presume that an overdrive that is slow to come in is suffering a worn pump and requires a complete overhaul. Repairs involve taking the engine and gearbox out and are costly, plus, 9 times out of 10, require the fitting of a new clutch. Try the same test in third gear, too, if your car is 1976 or earlier (on post-1976 cars, overdrive only worked on 'top' gear).

The overdrive units look like this, and are located at the rear of the gearbox.

Performance assessment

4 3 2 1

There are seven things to think about –

- Was the car idling comfortably at 800/850rpm?
- How did it go/sound generally, and did the engine rev willingly up to about 4500rpm?
- Did you spot any smoke from the exhaust when changing gear? If so, pop round

the back and take a fresh look at the rear bumper and back valance where any serious exhaust fumes could be deposited. This might signal a rich mixture or a worn engine.

• Did the car accelerate reasonably briskly and feel as if, in the right circumstances, it was a 100mph sports car? Try putting the throttle to the floor at about 1000rpm in top gear while listening for pinging/pinking that suggests excessively advanced timing, which can cause engine damage.

• Try climbing a modest hill at 50mph in top gear with the absolute minimum of throttle opening. Does the engine snatch, hesitate, cough or spit back? – any or all of which can signal a lean mixture and, possibly, worn throttle spindles (check later).

• Chrome bumper cars are prone to 'running-on/dieseling' on switching off the engine until the fuel in the carburettors is exhausted or you stall the car via the transmission. Later cars had anti-run-on valves fitted and should not be prone to the problem. If evident, running-on could signal incorrect plugs, excessive compression ratio, the need for a de-coke, the presence of higher octane fuel, or faulty anti-run-on valve(s).

• Rubber bumper cars became progressively burdened with emissions control equipment, particularly US ones – the function of which can be checked by starting off in first gear and revving the engine to 5000rpm+ before changing into second. Excessive fuel popping in the exhaust suggests blocked or faulty emissions equipment, or an overly rich carburettor(s) setting. The latter might be an effort to compensate for worn throttle spindles, which you should check for later.

Warm start

4 3 2 1

Does the car start well/quickly after standing a short while, and does the starter pinion engage every time, first time? If not, it could indicate a worn starter dog, or worse, that teeth are missing from the flywheel ring.

Steering – three checks

• Does the car steer straight (hands-off the wheel) when required?

• Does the steering self-centre after cornering – yes is good, no suggests partially seized, and thus poorly maintained, kingpins and front suspension.

• Is there any shaking of the steering wheel at 50, 60 or 70mph, suggesting that the front wheels need balancing? This symptom could also signal wear in the front suspension/dampers.

Front shocks

4 3 2 1

Assess their operation on a twisting and/or bumpy stretch of road.

Foot brake operation – five important checks

• Do the brakes inspire confidence,and can they be applied without excessive pedal travel (which could suggest general wear, badly adjusted rear brakes, and/or a lack of maintenance)?

• Do they stop the car in a straight line? If not, a caliper piston could be partially seized.

• Are there any scraping noises that suggest worn pads or rear linings? Presume new discs or drums will also be necessary.
• Check the master cylinder seals (particularly if the car has dual circuit hydraulics) by repeated, gentle, staccato application of the brakes with the car stationary. A good master cylinder will hardly allow the pedal position to change, while a suspect one will allow the pedal position to slowly sink towards the floor. This condition should be rectified immediately!
• Does the car have a brake servo fitted? If so, less pedal effort may justify an 'Excellent' award.

The front brake pads are easy to get at and change – provided the disc/rotor remains unscored.

Access to, replacement, and cost of the rear shoes is reasonable, assuming the drums are in good condition.

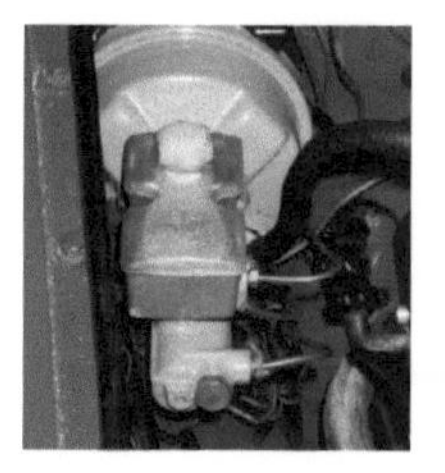

Rubber bumper and some earlier US cars had this close-coupled servo fitted to the driver's side of the engine bay.

Chrome bumper cars had a remote servo fitted over the passenger footwell.

Hand/parking brake 4 3 2 1

• Does it hold the car securely on a slight incline? If so, try it on a steep hill. Alternatively, pull on the handbrake and try to drive off in first gear. Forward progress suggests contaminated linings and/or out of adjustment and/or seized mechanism – all of which, sadly, are common MGB faults.

The brake adjuster for this side of the car is at '11 o'clock'.

There are other places the handbrake can seize, but this pivot is the usual one.

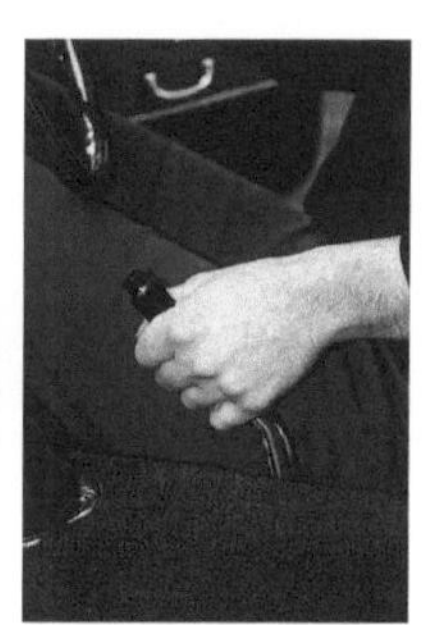

By now this handbrake should be securely 'on'.

• A properly adjusted handbrake should click up four, no more than five, notches on the ratchet.
• Allow the car to 'coast' down a slight incline after you've let off the handbrake – reluctance suggests 'binding' in the mechanism.
• Some of the late rubber bumper models produced between 1976 to 1980 have the potential for a bizarre problem that is the consequence of a faulty diode. This should allow electrical current to flow in one direction only. Test it by having the

engine running and by applying the handbrake with the central release button 'in' (as is good practice). If the starter motor engages, the diode is faulty and will need to be located, in the electrical harness behind the glovebox, and replaced.

The diode in question can be found behind the glove pocket of rubber bumper cars.

The rear axle – three tests 4 3 2 1

• Check the security of the rear axle by accelerating (hard) in second gear to about 4000rpm, then lift your foot off the accelerator/gas pedal without touching the brakes. If the car 'steers' to one side or the other, the rear axle securing U-bolts and spring pads are loose and/or worn. The rear springs could be faulty, but this is unlikely if the car was noted as standing flat/level in an earlier check.
• Listen for differential whine/wowing as you switch from power-on at, say, 50mph in top gear, to over-run. Try to induce it several times.
• The differential is prone to wearing the (plant gear) thrust washers, which results in a 'clunk' when you switch from power-on to over-run. Try several times in succession at about 40mph in third gear. The noise could also emanate from wheel splines (wire-wheel cars only), worn universal joints in the prop shaft, or worn half shafts, and might be best checked out by an expert if noted.

These U-bolts are loose because they're in the course of replacement. Yours should be secure.

Instruments/warning lights 4 3 2 1

This check is primarily to establish that they all work well. Neither the speedo nor tacho needles should waiver unduly. The ignition light should go out as engine revs build; oil pressure should not fade as water temperature increases. Furthermore, take this opportunity to assess what the instruments tell you about the car (e.g. does the oil pressure suggest an engine in good or poor condition; does the water temperature steadily rise suggesting an ineffective radiator or an engine that is generating too much heat?).

Dashboard switches and instruments 4 3 2 1

• With the engine running check that the respective switches operate the heater fan (two speed on most cars), internal light, wipers (two speed on most), lights and electric screen washers on later cars. If you're viewing a car with the manual, push-button washers, test them once and then again as late in the test as you can.
• The stalk controls varied greatly from model-to-model but check the function of those fitted to the car you are viewing.

Brake servo (if fitted) 4 3 2 1

As you finish the road test, check the servo is operating by switching off the engine, and placing your foot on the brake pedal, whereupon you should hear a 'chuff' noise. Operate the brakes a couple of times and then, with your foot still on the pedal, re-start the engine. You should feel the pedal depress if your servo is working satisfactorily. No chuff and/or no depression, and you should begin to question the servo's effectiveness.

Engine health

4 3 2 1

When you get out of the car, leave the engine running and check:

• That the exhaust is not puffing out smoke – black signals a worn engine or a very rich mixture, while white smoke requires you check for a blown head gasket.

• Undo the oil filler cap from the rocker cover and look at the underside. If covered in thick and black oil, the car may not have been maintained as you would wish. If emulsified with water, you have a head gasket problem. Brown slimy sludge can warn of general wear, while white foam suggests faulty evaporative loss control.

• Check the dipstick for water in the form of whitish emulsification droplets, which would indicate head gasket problems.

• BE VERY CAREFUL if the engine is still hot and the system pressurised, but it is prudent to remove the radiator cap as soon as you can to check the coolant level and cleanliness, and that it is oil-free. Cars with expansion tanks will also require the cap in the thermostat housing to be unscrewed once the system pressure has been 'let down' via the radiator pressure cap. Rusty water suggests poor maintenance, and an oil film suggests head gasket problems.

Mechanical aspects

Engine bay – 9 checks

4 3 2 1

• Does the external appearance of the radiator and water hoses suggest leaks (streaks of antifreeze) or loss of integrity?

• Although not fitted to very early UK cars, the vast majority of MGBs had an oil cooler, which were sometimes removed if they started to leak. Is yours in place?

• The time has finally come to check the carburettor throttle spindle(s) for wear. You should open the throttle about halfway (to allow

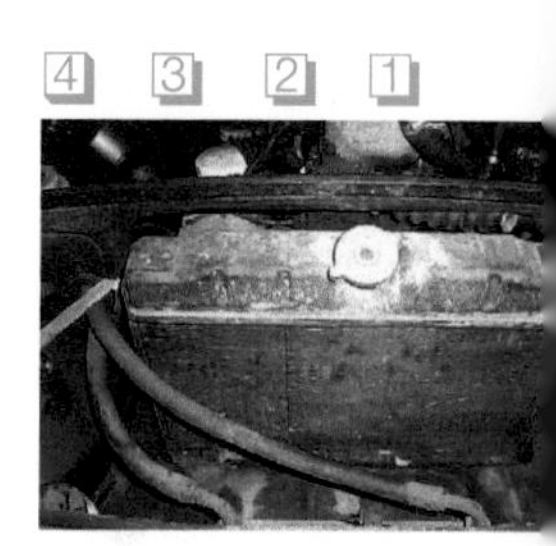

You would be unwise to buy this car and travel far before changing the radiator and water hoses.

The rubber bumper cars had the oil cooler slung under the radiator duct, but on chrome bumper cars the cooler sits over the radiator duct, as we see here.

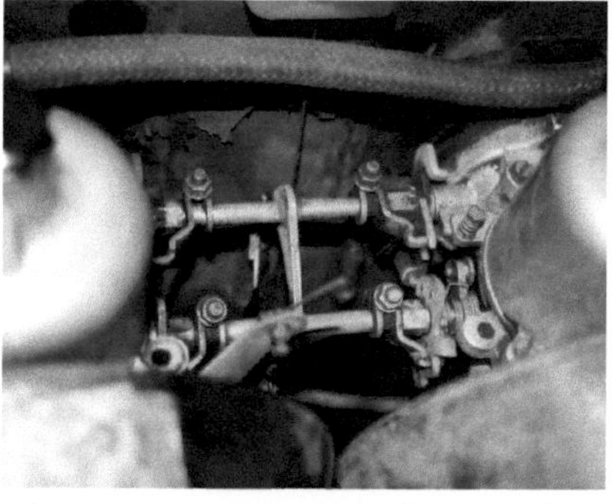

This is where you push/pull and test for play in the throttle spindle shaft ...

... and this is what you will need to fit if you find wear.

These are original air cleaners, exhaust manifold/header and rocker cover for a chrome bumper car. The air cleaners had curved inlets on later cars.

the butterfly to clear the body) and push/pull the spindle(s) in all directions. If movement is evident the spindles are worn and will need to be replaced.

• If originality is important check the air cleaners, exhaust manifold/header, and rocker cover (usual upgrades, which I personally would welcome).

• Look for oil leaks generally, and the condition of the oil pressure gauge capillary line where it is secured to the footwell (very prone to corrosion).

• Check that the flexible fuel lines and fastenings are in good order. Original rubber hoses are bad news in these days of 'aggressive' lead-free fuels, and the lines should clearly have been replaced in recent years – mark 'Excellent' if they're the stainless braided type.

• Not all MGBs left the factory with a fuel filter. By now, though, one should be in place in the fuel line adjacent to the bulkhead/firewall, and it should be clean, too!

• Not always easy to get at, but if the car is fitted with electric cooling fan(s) take a moment to check that it/they spin freely.

• Look down both sides of the engine at the flexible rubber engine mountings. Check whether they are cracked and, if in doubt, start the engine and re-check with the engine running.

The early MGBs were fitted with a fan mounted on the water pump; later cars had one or two electric fans like these.

The wiring loom – three checks

4 3 2 1

• The wiring loom must be secured neatly to the shell and not be chafed. The wires to the distributor get hot, which embrittles the insulation, but this should not be cracked. Take a good look at all non-original (usually unwrapped) wires that may have been added by previous owners for security alarms,

The fusebox is the heart of electrical reliability, and needs careful scrutiny for chafed, blackened and/or unsecured wires.

extra lights, etc. If they have secondary insulation, follow secure routes to their destination, use appropriate auto wires and colours, then all may be well. However, amateur installations are often positive dangers to the car and should be viewed with scepticism.

• There should be a two-position (later cars had a four-position) fusebox on the inner wing/fender with a cover.

• The gearbox loom (carries reverse lights, an overdrive inhibitor and, on automatics, the starter inhibitor) should be secured to the top mounting bolt for the starter motor. To my mind, the originality issue is not as important as the prevention of chafing to the harness.

Unleaded fuel conversion

4 3 2 1

Ask to see proof that the cylinder head has been converted to use unleaded fuel. This involves machining away the original valve seats away, and replacing them with hardened inserts, new valves, and phosphor bronze valve guides, and would be an unwelcome expense after you had bought the car.

Engine and chassis number check

While you've got your head in the engine bay, write down the engine number, check that the chassis plate is correctly positioned, and record the prefix and chassis number. Crosscheck the numbers and prefixes with the vendor's ownership documentation and the information shown in Chapter 17. The chassis/VIN plate position varied by year and by country, and your local club/chapter might be the best source of ensuring that the plate location is correct for your car.

Internal aesthetics

You shouldn't buy or reject a car on the basis of its hood, carpets and internal lining panels. A poor car beautifully trimmed is not a good buy, whilst a sound car with tatty trim is worth purchasing at the right price. Eight checks are worthwhile:

• Erect the hood, partly to ensure the frame is complete (pack-away) and not seized or bent, and partly to check for tears, cracks and the condition of the rear window (the latter is prone to cracking and clouding). On GTs fitted with a full length sunroof, check the fabric for cracking.

• Is a hood or a tonneau cover supplied? If a tonneau, does the zip slide easily over its full length?

• If fitted, pull sharply on both inertia seat belts to establish they lock properly.

• Check that the windows wind up and down reasonably smoothly.

• The carpets are quick and easy to replace, but should be in mint condition to warrant an 'Excellent' mark. Are the footwell carpets stuck to the floor (they must be removable)? Does the car have sound deadening felt fitted? Are the felts stuck to the floor or the underside of the carpet (mark down if stuck to the floor). Are supplementary floor mats fitted? If a replacement set of carpets is required, budget for the moulded, more expensive but infinitely preferable, options.

• The internal trim includes a number of vinyl-covered panels, by far the most important of which are the door panels. Are all the trim panels in place and in

The quality of the chrome is never more important on a chrome bumper car than on the bumpers themselves.

acceptable condition? Do the door panels look as if they have suffered water damage? Are all door fittings/furniture in place and in good order?
• Is the original steering wheel on the car? If an aftermarket wheel is fitted, is the original MGB wheel supplied with the car? If so, is it in good condition? (early originals are now in short supply).
• Are all the instruments in place, correct for the year of the car and looking good? Are the dashboard, trim and padding unmarked and uncracked? Strong sunlight can cause them to disintegrate.

External aesthetics – six checks

  2 

• You should have noted any stone chips or wiper scratches on the windscreen/windshield during your road test, but what about scratches on the side glasses, particularly on the driver's side, and chips from the top of the door windows?
• If you're after a top quality car, you should be looking at external brightwork with a critical eye. Replacement chrome bumpers are available, but are not up to the quality standard of the originals, so good original bumpers will be important to potential concours entrants. A rusted chrome finish can be repaired (at some expense) but holed, accident-damaged, and bent bumpers present a problem, and should be marked severely. New rubber bumpers are not available, but plenty of used ones are.
• Your MGB was originally fitted with 14in disc, Rostyle or wire wheels. Time, kerbs/curbs and salt damage all of them, but wires suffer the added hazard of broken or loose spokes if over-enthusiastically used. Check the outer faces and spokes (if applicable) for corrosion and damage. Personally, I would only mark 'Excellent' (unless you plan concours competition) if a set of attractive-looking alloy (ideally 5) wheels have been fitted.
• The condition of the tyres has important safety implications – so check the full-width tread on the road wheels, the brand (never heard of them, or a well-known brand?) and side-wall appearance. Mark very cautiously if side-wall cracking/crazing is evident (a consequence of longevity but little use).
• A full set of keys should be available. Check whether there is a duplicate set, that the same key works in both door locks, and that the boot/trunk and glove pocket locks perform.
• The boot/trunk should contain a road-legal spare wheel/tyre, a jack, a wheel brace and some basic tools.

Roadworthiness test certificate

MoT in the UK; TUV or DEKRA test in Germany; Controle Technique in France; while in the US individual states set (or in some cases do not set) their own test requirements. You need to see the most recent roadworthiness (and where applicable, emissions) certification for the car, and mark this section according to the outstanding period of validity.

Evaluation procedure

Add up the total points scored.
180 points = first-class, possibly concours; 135 points = good/very good;
90 points = average; 45 points = poor.
A car scoring over 126 should be completely usable and require the minimum of repair, although continued maintenance and care will be required to keep it in condition. Cars scoring between 45 and 92 points will require a full restoration – the cost of which will be much the same regardless of points scored. Cars scoring between 93 and 125 points will require very careful assessment of the necessary repair/restoration costs in order to arrive at a realistic purchase value.

10 Auctions

– sold! Another way to buy your dream

Auction pros & cons

Pros: Auctions are where dealers buy and sell, so they operate as trade rather than retail markets. This means that except for the so-called 'Prestige' auctions, prices are often lower than those on dealer premises and from some private sellers, so you could grab a bargain on the day. Auctioneers have usually confirmed ownership title with the seller and it should be possible to check this and any other relevant paperwork at the venue. You may also receive 24 hours of warranty cover.

Cons: You can normally only get either minimal information before travelling to the venue, or vague and sometimes very sales-orientated descriptions. To avoid disappointment, learn to read between the lines of the catalogue or website description and only visit if there are several candidate cars. Star lots may be stored indoors under good light, but even so, there is limited scope to examine the cars thoroughly. The wise buyer gets to the venue early and will do well to take this book, a mirror and a torch. Classic cars cannot be road tested, so for nearby venues try to arrive early on any preview days to see the lots arriving and being off-loaded or marshalled into position. The attendants may also be prepared to start up a car for you to hear it running. Intended as trade sales, the cars often need valeting, which dealers are happy to do and should not put you off.

Do your research, decide your personal limit and stick to it. Don't forget to budget for the auctioneer's charges to buyers as well as sellers, or the extra 5-10% may come as a shock. Admission is normally by catalogue and usually covers two people, so take a friend as it's amazing what a second pair of eyes can spot.

Catalogue prices and payment details

Auction catalogues and websites normally feature an estimated price and will spell out all charges and acceptable payment methods. Be sure you can comply before bidding. An immediate part-payment or deposit is usually requested if you win, with the balance payable within 24 hours. Check for cash and credit card limits, if any, and options such as personal cheques and debit cards or bankers. The car won't be released until all costs are cleared, with storage normally at your expense until the process is completed.

Viewing

In some instances it's possible to view the day before as well as the hours before an auction. Staff or owners may unlock doors, engine and luggage compartments for inspection or start the engine. Crawling around the car is fine but you may not jack up a vehicle – hence the need for a mirror on a stick.

Bidding

Before you take part in the auction, decide your maximum bid – and stick to it!

It may take a while for the auctioneer to reach the lot you are interested in, so use that time to observe how other bidders behave. When it's the turn of your vehicle, attract the auctioneer's attention and make an early bid. The auctioneer will then look to you for a reaction every time another bid is made, usually the bids will be in fixed increments until the bidding slows, when smaller increments will often be accepted before the hammer falls. If you want to withdraw from the bidding, make sure the auctioneer understands your intentions – a vigorous shake of the head when he or she looks to you for the next bid should do the trick.

Assuming that you are the successful bidder, the auctioneer will note your card or paddle number, and from that moment on you will be responsible for the vehicle.

If the MGB is unsold, either because it failed to reach the reserve or because there was little interest, it may be possible to negotiate with the owner, via the auctioneers, after the sale is over.

Successful bid

There are two more items to think about. How to get the MGB home, and insurance. If you can't drive the car, your own or a hired trailer is one way, another is to have the vehicle shipped using the facilities of a local company. The auction house will also have details of companies specialising in the transfer of all types of vehicles.

Insurance for immediate cover can usually be purchased on site, but it may be more cost-effective to make arrangements in advance (don't forget classic vehicle insurance).

eBay & other online auctions

eBay and other online auctions could land you an MGB at a bargain price, though you'd be foolhardy to bid without examining the vehicle first, something most vendors encourage. A useful feature of eBay is that the geographical location of the vehicle is shown, so you can narrow your choices to those within a realistic radius of home. Be prepared to be outbid in the last few moments of the auction. Remember, your bid is binding, and it will be very, very difficult to get restitution in the case of a crooked vendor fleecing you – caveat emptor!

Be aware that some vehicles offered for sale in online auctions are 'ghost' vehicles. Don't part with any cash without being sure that the car does actually exist and is as described (usually pre-bidding inspection is possible).

Auctioneers

Barrett-Jackson www.barrett-jackson.com
Bonhams www.bonhams.com
British Car Auctions (BCA) www.bca-europe.com or www.british-car-auctions.co.uk
Cheffins www.cheffins.co.uk
Christies www.christies.com
Coys www.coys.co.uk
eBay www.ebay.com or www.ebay.co.uk
H&H www.classic-auctions.co.uk
RM www.rmauctions.com
Shannons www.shannons.com.au
Silver www.silverauctions.co

11 Paperwork

– correct documentation is essential!

The paper trail

Classic, collector and prestige cars usually come with a large portfolio of paperwork accumulated and passed on by a succession of proud owners. This documentation represents the real history of the car and from it can be deduced the level of care the car has received, how much it's been used, which specialists have worked on it and the dates of major repairs and restorations. All of this information will be priceless to you as the new owner, so be very wary of cars with little paperwork to support their claimed history.

Registration documents

All countries/states have some form of registration for private vehicles whether its like the American 'pink slip' system or the British 'log book' system.

It is essential to check that the registration document is genuine, that it relates to the car in question, and that all the vehicle's details are correctly recorded, including chassis/VIN and engine numbers (if these are shown). If you are buying from the previous owner, his or her name and address will be recorded in the document: this will not be the case if you are buying from a dealer.

In the UK the current (Euro-aligned) registration document is named 'V5C,' and is printed in coloured sections of blue, green and pink. The blue section relates to the car specification, the green section has details of the new owner and the pink section is sent to the DVLA in the UK when the car is sold. A small section in yellow deals with selling the car within the motor trade.

Previous ownership records

Due to the introduction of important new legislation on data protection, it is no longer possible to acquire, from the British DVLA, a list of previous owners of a car you own, or are intending to purchase. This scenario will also apply to dealerships and other specialists, from who you may wish to make contact and acquire information on previous ownership and work carried out.

If the car has a foreign registration, there may be expensive and time-consuming formalities to complete. Do you really want the hassle?

Roadworthiness certificate

Most country/state administrations require that vehicles are regularly tested to prove that they are safe to use on the public highway and do not produce excessive emissions. In the UK that test (the 'MOT') is carried out at approved testing stations, for a fee. In the USA the requirement varies, but most states insist on an emissions test every two years as a minimum, while the police are charged with pulling over unsafe-looking vehicles.

In the UK the test is required on an annual basis once a vehicle becomes three years old. Of particular relevance for older cars is that the certificate issued includes the mileage reading recorded at the test date and, therefore, becomes an independent record of that car's history. Ask the seller if previous certificates are available. Without an MOT the vehicle should be trailered to its new home, unless you insist that a valid MOT is part of the deal. (Not such a bad idea this, as at least you will know the car was roadworthy on the day it was tested and you don't need to wait for the old certificate to expire before having the test done.)

In the UK, vehicles over 40 years old on May 20th each year, are exempt from MOT testing. Owners can still have the test carried out if they so wish.

Road licence

The administration of every country/state charges some kind of tax for the use of its road system, the actual form of the 'road licence' and, how it is displayed, varying enormously country to country and state to state.

Whatever the form of the road licence, it must relate to the vehicle carrying it and must be present and valid if the car is to be driven on the public highway legally.

Changed legislation in the UK means that the seller of a car must surrender any existing road fund licence, and it is the responsibility of the new owner to re-tax the vehicle at the time of purchase and before the car can be driven on the road. It's therefore vital to see the Vehicle Registration Certificate (V5C) at the time of purchase, and to have access to the New Keeper Supplement (V5C/2), allowing the buyer to obtain road tax immediately.

In the UK, classic vehicles 40 years old or more on the 1st January each year get free road tax. It is still necessary to renew the tax status every year, even if there is no change.

If the car is untaxed because it has not been used for a period of time, the owner has to inform the licensing authorities.

Certificates of authenticity

For many makes of collectible car it is possible to get a certificate proving the age and authenticity (eg engine and chassis numbers, paint colour and trim) of a particular vehicle. These are sometimes called 'Heritage Certificates' and if the car comes with one of these it is a definite bonus. If you want to obtain one, the relevant owner's club is the best starting point.

If the car has been used in european classic car rallies it may have a FIVA (Federation Internationale des Vehicules Anciens) certificate. The so-called 'FIVA Passport,' or 'FIVA Vehicle Identity Card,' enables organisers and participants to recognise whether or not a particular vehicle is suitable for individual events. If you want to obtain such a certificate go to www.fbhvc.co.uk or www.fiva.org. There will be similar organisations in other countries.

Valuation certificate

Hopefully, the vendor will have a recent valuation certificate, or letter signed by a recognised expert stating how much he, or she, believes the particular car to be worth (such documents, together with photos, are usually needed to get 'agreed value' insurance). Generally, such documents should act only as confirmation of your own assessment of the car rather than a guarantee of value as the expert has probably not seen the car in the flesh. The easiest way to find out how to obtain a formal valuation is to contact one of the specialist suppliers listed in Chapter 16.

Service history

Often these cars will have been serviced at home by enthusiastic (and hopefully capable) owners for a good number of years. Nevertheless, try to obtain as much service history and other paperwork pertaining to the car as you can. Naturally, dealer stamps, or specialist garage receipts, score most points in the value stakes.

However, anything helps in the great authenticity game: items like the original bill of sale, handbook, parts invoices and repair bills, adding to the story and character of the car. Even a brochure from the year of the car's manufacture is a useful document, and something that you could well have to search hard for in future years. If the seller claims that the car has been restored, expect receipts and other evidence from a specialist restorer.

If the seller claims to have carried out regular servicing, ask what work was completed, when, and seek some evidence of it being done. Your assessment of the car's overall condition should tell you whether the seller's claims are genuine.

Restoration photographs

If the seller tells you that the car has been restored, then expect to be shown a series of photographs taken while the restoration was under way. Pictures taken at various stages, and from various angles, should help you gauge the thoroughness of the work. If you buy the car, ask if you can have all the photographs as they form an important part of the vehicle's history. It's surprising how many sellers are happy to part with their car and accept your cash, but want to hang on to their photographs! In the latter event, you may be able to persuade the vendor to get a set of copies made.

12 What's it worth?

– let your head rule your heart

Condition

If the car you've been looking at is really bad, then you've probably not bothered to use the marking system in Chapter 9 (the 60 minute evaluation). You may not have even got as far as using that chapter at all! If you did use the marking system you'll know whether the car is in Excellent (maybe Concours), Good, Average or Poor condition, or, perhaps, somewhere in-between. This information should enable you to use one of the many classic/collector car magazines that run a price guide.

If you haven't bought the latest issues, do so now and compare their suggested values for the model you're thinking of buying: also look at the auction prices they're reporting. Values have been fairly stable for some time, but some models will always be more sought-after than others. Trends can change, too. The values published in the magazines tend to vary from one magazine to another, as do their scales of condition, so carefully read the guidance notes provided. Bear in mind that a car which is truly a recent show winner could be worth more than the highest scale published. Assuming that the car you have in mind is not in show/concours condition, relate the level of condition that you judge the car to be in with the appropriate guide price. How does the figure compare with the asking price? Before you start haggling with the seller, consider what affect any variation from standard specification might have on the car's value.

If you're buying from a dealer, there will be a dealer's premium on the price. Negotiate on the basis of condition, mileage, and fault rectification cost. Take into account the car's specification. Be realistic about the value, but don't be completely intractable; a small compromise on the part of the vendor or buyer will often facilitate a deal at little real cost.

Desirable options/extras

Wire wheels, preferably chrome finished. Failing that, 5.5J alloy wheels.
Most MGB enthusiasts generally prefer chrome bumper models although the rubber bumper models are the later cars and this sometimes attracts buyers on the basis that they are thought to be the more reliable.
Overdrive on the gearbox.
Telescopic rear damper conversion.
Brake servo.
Polyurethane suspension bushes.
Electric fan conversion.
Tubular exhaust manifolds and sports exhaust system.
Electronic ignition conversion.
Upgraded front suspension incorporating telescopic dampers.
Mohair hood.
Enlarged engine capacity, provided the work can be shown to have been carried out by a reputable company.

Undesirable features

Chrome bumper conversions from rubber bumper cars.
Non-original colour.
Fibreglass body panels.
Originality enthusiasts would prefer an original steering wheel, particularly on a very early car.

13 Do you really want to restore?

– it'll take longer and cost more than you think

There is a lot going for any practical enthusiast who wants to restore an MGB. Firstly, the bodyshell is an integral unit, which means if yours is beyond your own refurbishment ability or economic restoration by specialists, you can simply buy a new one. This makes the restoration of an MGB little more than a re-assembly project if you so wish. Secondly, if you want to try restoring your original shell, the replacement panels are all available and the 'fit' of the replacement body panels is generally very good, which means you don't have to have years of body repair experience to tackle an MGB restoration. Furthermore, parts availability is excellent, and the car is basically a simple vehicle that enables many enthusiasts from all walks of life to carry out superb restorations.

It's a good idea to buy a Heritage bodyshell pre-painted in the colour of your choice. After delivery it is then a matter of whether you transfer the parts as they are from the old to the new shell (and will likely be disappointed at the end of the exercise), or you refurbish everything along the way, in which case you should end up with a superb car like this with nothing more than assembly skills, patience and a cheque book!

So, restoring an MGB is not impractical by any means. Nevertheless, it is a sad but inescapable fact that all too frequently the owner fails to complete the restoration project. Often the incomplete car then forms the basis for 'abandoned project' entries in the 'For sale' columns, or the final stages are rushed so that the car can be sold. Furthermore, even in a well-executed complete restoration, the owner rarely recovers costs.

One reason many home restorations stop short of completion is that the owner underestimates the volume of work or the timescale involved. Sometimes the car appears to want nothing much more than a little care and attention – but things are ALWAYS worse, usually far worse than the unsuspecting owner ever imagined. He removes a wing/fender and finds tin-worm everywhere – whereupon things go from bad to worse. One MGB I bought in thousands of pieces had, about 5 years before, been suffering with

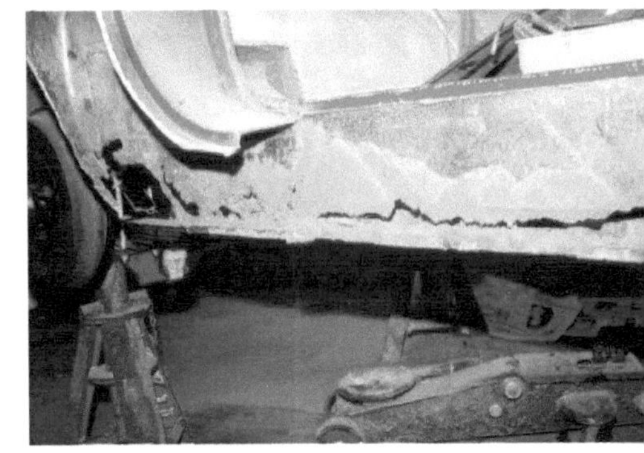

The sills/rockers on any car are important to its structural integrity, but in an open sports car like an MGB they are vital to your safety ... and they are ALWAYS far worse than you expect!

a slipping clutch. Out came the engine and gearbox but both revealed unexpected wear, and both were stripped for rectification. Frankly, I am not sure how this progressed to starter and wiper motors, to the front wings, and even the sills/rockers – but the car ended up in dozens of boxes and quite beyond the owner's capability to repair and re-assemble. So you also need to ask yourself whether you have the technical competence to undertake a full restoration and the strength of character to seek help if things start to get out of hand.

Do you have the cleaning, repairing and re-painting patience to cope with the hundreds of parts involved in a full restoration? What about the skill to put the parts back together in the right order?

Then, I guess, you need to ask yourself whether you have the finances to seek professional help if and when needed. Probably the single most frequent reason for incomplete restoration projects is that the cost proves more than was initially envisaged, followed fairly closely by the work taking far longer than was expected. Even for the experienced, the cost and timescale are ALWAYS more than expected!

The technical, cost and time issues are largely trade-offs. The more technically competent you are, the more you can do yourself. The more you can do yourself the less the project should cost, but the longer it will take.

Mind you, there are other reasons why projects become abandoned. Insufficient space, tools, and workshop facilities are all contributory factors. Did you appreciate that a disassembled MGB takes up about three times the space of an assembled one? What about the welding set, benders, hand tools, lighting, heating, and location where you can bash away in the evening without the neighbours and/or the wife getting upset?

Even before you buy a 'restoration project' car, prepare for and plan the restoration very carefully. Most people only carry out one restoration in their lives, so look through Chapter 16 and seek advice from club members who have done it, read the relevant books, and talk to the professionals before you start. Where something can be postponed for a year or two (e.g. perhaps an engine rebuild) do so. Where you have to get the whole job done thoroughly first time (e.g. body panel repairs and paint spraying) be sure you do even if it necessitates using professionals for that part of the project.

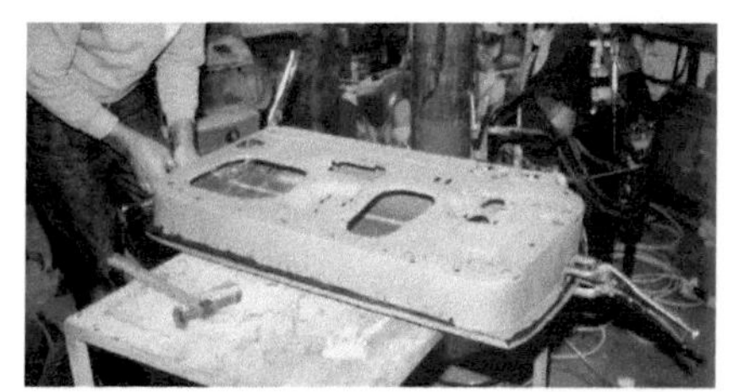

You can buy new doors in preference to the re-skinning that is taking place here – but they still have to be fitted.

You need space – ideally (a lot) more space than I had here.

14 Paint problems

– bad complexion, including dimples, pimples and bubbles

Paint faults generally occur due to lack of protection/maintenance, or poor preparation prior to a respray or touch-up. Some of the following conditions may be present in the car you're looking at:

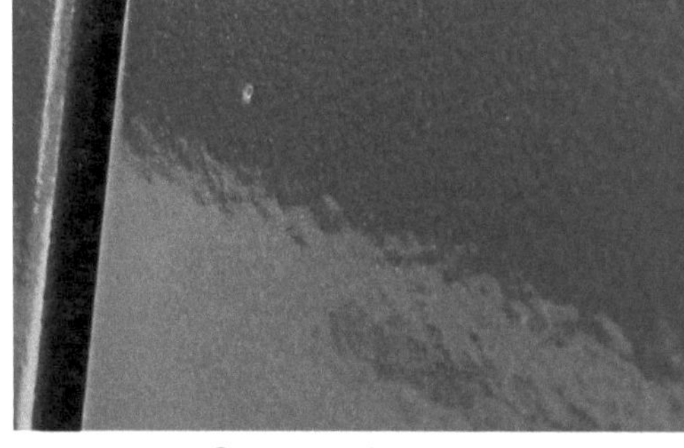

Orange peel.

Orange peel

This appears as an uneven paint surface, similar in appearance to the skin of an orange. The fault is caused by the failure of atomized paint droplets to flow into each other when they hit the surface. It's sometimes possible to rub out the effect with proprietary paint cutting/rubbing compound or very fine grades of abrasive paper. A respray may be necessary in severe cases. Consult a bodywork repairer/paint shop for advice on the particular car.

Cracking

Severe cases are likely to have been caused by too heavy an application of paint (or filler beneath the paint). Also, insufficient stirring of the paint before application can result in the components being improperly mixed, and cracking can result. Incompatibility with the paint already on the panel can have a similar effect. To rectify the problem it is necessary to rub down to a smooth, sound finish before respraying the problem area.

Crazing

Sometimes the paint takes on a crazed rather than a cracked appearance when the problems mentioned under 'Cracking' are present. This problem can also be caused by a reaction between the underlying surface and the paint. Paint removal and respraying the problem area is usually the only solution.

Rust blistering ...

Blistering

Almost always caused by corrosion of the metal beneath the paint. Usually perforation will be found in the metal and the damage will usually be worse than that suggested by the area of blistering. The metal will have to be repaired before repainting.

Micro blistering

Usually the result of an economy respray where inadequate heating has allowed moisture to settle on the car before spraying. Consult a paint specialist, but usually damaged paint will have to be removed before partial or full respraying. Can also be caused by car covers that don't 'breathe.'

Fading

Some colours, especially reds, are prone to fading if subjected to strong sunlight for long periods without the benefit of polish protection. Sometimes proprietary paint restorers and/or paint cutting/rubbing compounds will retrieve the situation. Often a respray is the only real solution.

Peeling

Often a problem with metallic paintwork when the sealing laquer becomes damaged and begins to peel off. Poorly applied paint may also peel. The remedy is to strip and start again!

Dimples

Dimples in the paintwork are caused by the residue of polish (particularly silicone types) not being removed properly before respraying. Paint removal and repainting is the only solution.

Dents

Small dents are usually easily cured by the 'Dentmaster,' or equivalent process, that sucks or pushes out the dent (as long as the paint surface is still intact). Companies offering dent removal services usually come to your home: consult your telephone directory.

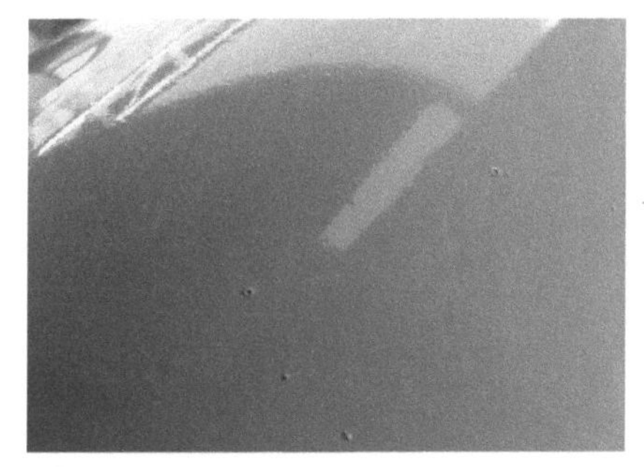

Dimples and orange peel.

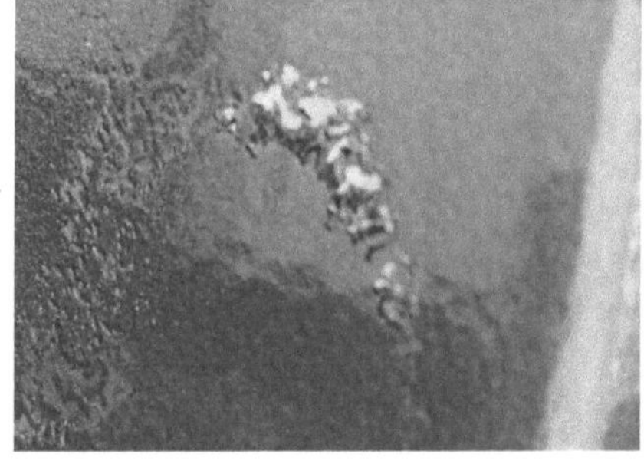

Reaction and rust blistering.

15 Problems due to lack of use

– just like their owners, cars need exercise!

Cars, like humans, need regular exercise. A run of at least ten miles, once a week, is recommended for classics if the conditions are dry and the car is taxed, MoTd and insured. If an actual run is impractical I suggest you start the car and use as many of its mechanical features as you can for 15 to 20 minutes once a month. This is particularly valuable if you have the rear wheels safely up on axle stands and can thus exercise the clutch, gearbox, overdrive, rear axle and brakes. Ensure the engine is used for long enough to open the thermostat, whereupon you should circulate the coolant with some vigour (i.e. do not leave the car idling) for a minimum of 5 minutes. I like 2500rpm for these warm-ups.

Check and, if necessary, inflate the tyres to running pressure. I would also disconnect the earth/ground terminal from the battery until time for another start-up, but connect a battery conditioner or trickle charger for a few hours after the car's periodic exercise.

Never leave the car unused with –

- the hand/parking brake 'on', as the shoes can rust to the drums and the cable seize/freeze.
- the weight of the car on the tyres. An unchanged position develops flat spots, resulting in (sometimes temporary) vibration. Furthermore, the tyre walls may crack or develop blister-type bulges, necessitating new tyres.
- weak or no antifreeze protection in the coolant. The corrosion inhibitors in antifreeze help prevent corroded internal waterways and, of course, also stop freezing which can cause core plugs to be pushed out, and even cracks in the block or head. Silt settling and solidifying can cause subsequent overheating.
- old/well-used engine oil in the sump/oil pan – the acid that builds up during combustion corrodes bearings.

Not only does this hand/parking brake pivot seize, but so too will the cable and backplate pivot.

Radiators and hoses can deteriorate in use, but insufficient anti-freeze will damage not only the radiator but possibly the engine, too, if the temperature in your region falls far enough.

When evaluating potential purchases bear in mind that, after long periods of inactivity, the following problems are also likely, depending upon the period of inactivity, storage conditions and pre-storage preparation –

- Pistons can seize in the cylinders due to corrosion.
- Pistons can corrode in the carburettor dashpot(s).

The first problem with inactive brakes is that the pads corrode to the disc/rotor. This is usually easily fixed, but corrosion between piston and caliper will probably require exchange calipers.

If the carburettors stand unused for a protracted period this piston will corrode into the dashpot housing, and the car will require the choke 'out' to run.

- Pistons in brake and clutch calipers, slave and master cylinders can seize.
- The bonnet/hood cable and catch can seize/freeze.
- The clutch may seize if the plate becomes stuck to the flywheel because of corrosion.
- Lip seals in the main working components stick to their respective shafts and can be damaged upon starting.
- Brake fluid absorbs water from the atmosphere and should be renewed every two years in any event. However, in storage conditions old fluid with a high water content can cause corrosion within the braking system and pistons/calipers to seize (freeze). This, in turn, can cause brake failure when the water turns to vapour near hot braking components.
- With lack of use, the shock absorbers/dampers will lose elasticity, or even seize. Creaking, groaning and stiff suspension are signs of this problem.
- Radiator hoses may have perished and split, possibly resulting in the loss of all coolant. Window and door seals can harden and leak. Gaitors/boots can crack. Wiper blades will harden.
- The battery will be of little use if it has not been charged for many months. Earthing/grounding problems are common when the connections have corroded. Old bullet and spade type electrical connectors commonly rust/corrode and will need disconnecting, cleaning and protection (with Vaseline, for example). Sparkplug electrodes will often have corroded in an unused engine. Wiring insulation can harden and fail.
- Mild steel exhaust systems corrode when a car is unused as the result of the water and combustion gasses trapped in the system. Expect non-stainless systems to have to be replaced as a matter of course as part of your re-commissioning costs.

16 The Community

– key people, organisations & companies in the MGB world

Clubs

UK

MG Owners Club, Swavesey, Cambridge CB4 5QZ, England. Tel: 01954 231125. Web: www.mgownersclub.co.uk.
MG Car Club, Kimber House, 12 Cemetery Road, Abingdon, Oxon, OX14 1AS England. Tel: 01235 555552.
Web: www.mgcc.co.uk.
MGB Registrar, Bernard Rengger, Tel: 01858 431271.
Email: secretary@mgb-register.org.

All the MGB focused clubs run numerous meetings and events throughout the year, bringing the MG community together. Park, polish and/ or socialise is probably the most popular. There is at least one each week. This line-up is mostly MGBs, but I see one MGC in attendance, too.

The meetings and social gatherings take place Stateside, too ... this is a line-up of 'LE' (Limited Edition) MGBs. Note the side 'repeater lights' in front wings/ fenders.

North America

North American MGB Register, Post Office Box 69, Eaton Rapids, MI 48827 USA. Tel: 800-NAMGBR-1. Web: www.mgcars.org.uk/namgbr.
Email: bcwyckoff@mindspring.com.

American MGB Association, PO Box 11401, Chicago IL 60611 USA.
Tel: 1-800-723-MGMG (6464). Web: www.mgcars.org.uk/amgba.
Email: info@mgclub.org.

Europe

MGCC Antwerp, Frits Van Den Berghelaan 150, B-2630 Aartselaar, Belgium. Email: mavro@skynet.be.
MGCC Belgium, Alain Van Langeraert, Flandrialaan 12, 8434 Westende, Belgium. Email: alain.vanlangeraert@skynet.be.
MGCC Bulgari, Rumen Raichev, MG-Rover-RIV-Club. mgroverclub@mail.bg.
MGCC Czech Republic Radek Pelc, K Vyzkumnym ustavum, 14220 Prague 4, Czech Republic. Email: mg-cars@post.cz.
MGCC Danish Centre, Lars Thausig Hyldestubben 8, 2730 Herlev, Denmark. Email: 1t.@mgklub.dk.
MGCC Denmark, Michael Elkjær, Kamgræsvej 7, 9800 Hjørring, Denmark.
Email: Michael@mgcc.dk .
MGCC Eire, Fred Lewis, Pineridge, Kilgobbin Road, Stepaside, Co Dublin, Ireland.
MGCC Finland, Merja Autio, Pistiäisentie 1 B, 01490 Vantaa, Finland.
Email: merja.autio@pp.inet.fi.

Park and polish takes on a new meaning when it comes to the numerous 'Condition' competitions that take place each year. These proud *Concours d'Elegance* winners took their Jubilee Special Edition of the MGB GT to an MG Car Club meeting at Stanford Hall.

My wife and I enjoy the locally organised runs, made usually in convoy, frequently incorporating a pause at a stately home, castle, scenic view or other place of interest. Often, such runs take us to parts of the county we've not previously seen, and most include a picnic lunch stop.

MGCC France, Christian Lissot, 8, rue de l'Étang, Le, Guay, 91460 Marcoussis, France. Email: lissots@wanadoo.fr.
MGCC Germany, Friedhelm Seifen, Schonebecker Hagen 17, D-28757 Bremen, Germany.
Email: sekretaer@mgcc.de.
MGCC Holland, Anka den Hollander, Vossegatselaan 56, 3583 RV Utrecht, Holland. Email: mgnieuws@mgcarclub.nl.
MGCC d'Italia, Fabio Filippello, Via Accademia dei Virtuosi 22, 00147 Roma.
Email: mgcarclub@mclink.it.
MGCC Luxembourg, Ton Maathuis, 1 Rue Tomm, L-9454 Fouhren, Luxembourg.
Email: mgcarclub@mgcarclub.lu.
MGCC Norway, Erik Kathrud, Arons vei 48, N-3029 Drammen, Norway.
Email: info@nmgk.no.
MAIA MGCC Portugal, Luis Pinho, Forum Jovem Da Maia, Tr Cruzes do Monte, 46, 4470-169 Maia Portugal.
Email: luis.pinho@netcabo.pt.
MGCC Monaco, Nicola Parolin, Columbus Hotel, 23, Avenue de Papalins, 98000 Monaco, Monaco Principality.
Email: info@mgcarclubmonaco.net.
MGCC Spain, Ferran Boix, Club MG CATALUNYA. c/ Apartado de Correos 90032 Barcelona-08080. Email: secreetaria@mg.catalunya.com.
MGCC Sweden, Harald Soneson, Vasbystrandsvagen 38, SE-184 95 Ljustero, Sweden.
Email: overseas@mgcc.se.
MGCC Switzerland, Jaques Merminod, Postfach, CH-4002, Basel, Switzerland.
Email: ausland@mgcc.ch.

Historic car rallying is fun at club level – i.e. before it gets very serious! These are some members of the MG Car Club at play.

UK main spares suppliers

Moss-Europe, Hampton Farm Estate, Hanworth, Middx, TW13 6DB, England. Tel: 020 8867 2020. Email: sales@moss-europe.co.uk.
MGB Hive, Marshalls Bank, Parsons Drove, Wisbech, Cambs, England. Tel: 01945 700500. Web: www.mgbhive.co.uk.

MG Owners Club Spares, Swavesey, Cambridge CB4 5QZ, England. Tel: 01954 230928. Email: sales@mgocspares.co.uk.
The Welsh MG Centre, Wrexham Road, Rhostyllen, Wrexham, LL14 4DW. Tel: 01978 351635. Web: www.welshmg.co.uk.

US main specialist spares suppliers

The Roadster Factory, PO Box 332, Killen Road, Armagh, PA 15920 USA. Tel: (800) 678-8764. Web: www.the-roadster-factory.com.
Victoria British Ltd, Box 14991, Lenexa, KS 66285-4991, USA. Tel: (800) 255-0088. Web: www.longmotor.com.
Moss Motors, PO Box 847, 440 Rutherford Street, Goleta, CA 93116, USA. Tel: (800) 667-7872. Web: www.mossmotors.com.

MG Car Club race meetings are popular, whether watching, supporting friends or competing – Druids Bend at Brands Hatch is always exciting, particularly the first time round.

Overdrive repair specialists

Overdrive Repair Services, Units C3/4 Ellisons Road, Norwood Industrial Estate, Killamarsh, Sheffield, S21 2JG England. Tel: 0114 2482632. Web: www.overdrive-repairs.co.uk/products.
Overdrive Spares, Unit A2 Wolston Business Park, Main Street, Wolston, Nr Coventry, CV8 3FU. England. Tel: 02476 543686. Email: odspares@aol.com.

Magazines & books

MG Enthusiast, Octane Media Ltd, Isis Way, Minerva Business Park, Peterborough, PE2 6QR. Web: www.mg-enthusiast.com.
MG Magazine, PO Box 321, Otego, NY 13825, USA. Web: www.mgcars.org.uk.
The Original MGB by Anders Ditler Clausager ISBN 1-870979-48-6.
Your Expert Guide to MGB & MGB GT problems & how to fix them by Roger Williams. Veloce Publishing. ISBN 1-903706-50-3.
MGB, The Complete Story by Brian Laban. ISBN 1-85223-358-3.
MGB Parts & Accessories Catalogue – Moss-Europe & Moss Motors (USA).
Guide to Purchase & DIY Restoration of the MGB by Lindsay Porter. ISBN 0-854296-64-6.
How to Improve MGB, MGC & MGB V8 by Roger Williams. Veloce Publishing. ISBN 1-901295-76-1.
How to Build & Power Tune Distributor-type Ignition Systems by Des Hammill. Veloce Publishing. ISBN 978-1-84584-186-7.
How to Power Tune MGB 4-cylinder Engines by Peter Burgess. Veloce Publishing. ISBN 978-1-903706-77-0.
How to give your MGB V8 power by Roger Williams. Veloce Publishing. ISBN 978-1-904788-93-5.

17 Vital statistics

– essential data at your fingertips

Production history

Mark I – 1962 to October 1967

September 1962: B Roadster launched at Earls Court Motor Show UK.
Car was fitted with 'pull-handles' until 1965, when the push-button handle was introduced and used for the remaining life of the car.
October 1964: 5-bearing engine introduced.
October 1965: GT launched.
April 1967: Salisbury rear axle fitted as standard to Roadster.
Chassis number prefix GHN3 (Roadster cars) and GHD3 (GT variant) for period 1962 to 1967 (Note: Some Mark I cars were built during 1968).
115,898 Roadsters and 21,835 GTs were built.

Mark II – November 1967 to October 1969

Launched fitted with all-synchomesh gearbox that stayed in use until production of the 'B' ceased in 1980.
These cars continued to use a vertical bar chrome radiator grille identical to that fitted to Mark I cars.
Chassis number prefixes G-HN4 (Roadster cars) and G-HD4 (GT variant) were used to identify the Mk IIs.
BL manufactured 31,767 Roadsters and 16,943 GTs.

Mark III – October 1969 to September 1974

Recessed black radiator grille introduced, and the chassis number prefix was changed to GHN5 and GHD5 for Roadsters and GTs respectively.
A face-lift in October 1971 featured a revised dashboard and vinyl seat covering (replacing the leather used previously). US cars employed additional padding and shape.
October 1972: A more traditional radiator grille re-introduced employing a conventional shaped aluminium surround fitted with a black plastic mesh backing.
110,643 Roadsters and 59,459 GTs were completed.

Rubber bumper cars – September 1974 to 1980

Rubber bumper variant launched incorporating several under-bonnet/hood panel changes, increased ride height, suspension changes, and a single 12-volt battery.
1976 second version of rubber bumper cars launched employing different trim, dashboard, a forward radiator position, and suspension changes to redress the poor handling of the original rubber bumper cars.
Chassis number prefixes were superseded by a VIN prefix for cars numbered 501001 and onwards in June 1979, when the 1980 model commenced production. Thus, the final cars were prefixed GVVDJ2A (a LHD US specification 1980 model Roadster) or GVGEJ1A (a UK GT).

Production ceased 23rd October 1980 after 128,653 Roadsters and 27,045 GTs had left the factory.

Additional information

- Chrome bumper car weights: Roadster 2080lb, GT 2308lb.
- An auto-boxed variant was available.
- In 1971 small cosmetic black buffers were fitted to all chrome bumper over-riders.
- 1974 USA exports were fitted with chrome bumpers as usual but large black solid rubber over-riders replaced the usual items. These were nicknamed 'Sabrina' over-riders.
- Factory reconditioned engines were prefixed 48G and, later, BHM.
- Original engine numbers had a wide range of prefixes, which distinguished between the high and low compression engines and units fitted with auto and manual gearboxes.
- Four-synchro boxes had two larger bearings fitted for additional longevity as well as the additional synchro on first gear.

Principle colours

The colours used during the 28-year production cycle of the MGB were too many and varied to list comprehensively here, but the following were probably the most popular and numerous.

Black	Used throughout the production run in two shades/code-numbers
Beiges & browns	Antilope
	Bronze (metallic)
	Harvest Gold
Blues	Bermuda
	Iris (light or 'powder') used on Mk I and Mk II Roadsters
	Midnight (very dark) used on Mk I, II & III cars
	Mineral (dark) used on Mk I and Mk II cars
	Royal (dark)
	Teal (mid) used 1971 to '74
	Tahiti (bright or 'electric' used 1975 to '76
Greens	Mallard (mid)
	British Racing used in two shades throughout all models
Greys	Chelsea (light) used on Mk I and Mk II Roadsters
	Grampian (mid)
Reds	Blaze
	Damask used on Mk II and Mk III cars
	Flame (bright mid shade with a tinge of orange)
	Tartan used on Mk I and Mk II
Whites	Glacier
	Old English used on Mk I and Mk II cars
	Leyland
Yellows	Citron
	Primrose used on Mk I and Mk II

Also from Veloce Publishing –

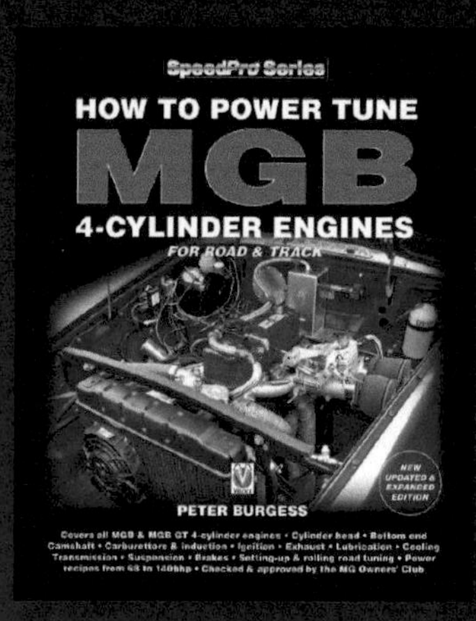

Paperback • 25x20.7cm
• 144 pages • 100 pictures
ISBN: 978-1-787113-41-1

SpeedPro Series
HOW TO BUILD, MODIFY
& POWER TUNE
CYLINDER
HEADS
UPDATED & REVISED EDITION
Peter Burgess & David Gollan

Paperback • 25x20.7cm
• 112 pages • 150+ pictures
ISBN: 978-1-903706-76-3

Paperback • 25x20.7cm
• 80 pages • 98 pictures
ISBN: 978-1-787111-73-8

Paperback • 25x20.7cm
• 64 pages • 95 pictures
ISBN: 978-1-903706-59-6

For more info on Veloce titles, visit our website at www.veloce.co.uk
email: info@veloce.co.uk • Tel: +44(0)1305 260068

The Essential Buyer's Guide™ series ...